T0113878

Moral and Ethical Issues:

Confronting Orthodox Christian Teens across North America

By

Joseph F. Purpura

© 1999, 2002 by Joseph F. Purpura. All rights reserved.

No part of this book may be reproduced, stored in a retrieval system, or transmitted by any means, electronic, mechanical, photocopying, recording, or otherwise, without written permission from the author.

ISBN: 978-1-4033-1666-0 (sc)
ISBN: 978-1-4033-1665-3 (e)

Print information available on the last page.

This book is printed on acid free paper.

1stBooks – rev. 03/26/2024

TABLE OF CONTENTS

ACKNOWLEDGMENT

Special thanks to the thousands of teens across the Antiochian Orthodox Christian Archdiocese of North America who have allowed me to enter into their lives over the past twenty years, to Mr. Raymond Yazge my first mentor in Youth Ministry, and to Metropolitan PHILIP, who has allowed me to minister to teens across the North American Continent.

Gratitude is expressed to Fr. Joseph Kimmett and Deacon Douglas Kevorkian for their help in proof reading this document, Paul Garrett for his assistance with database development and Professor Byron Jackson and the Very Rev. Joseph Allen for their extensive guidance and help with this work.

I thank my own children, my sons Michael, David, Christina and Jennifer for their patience with me through the years of my ministry.

I especially thank Kathleen, my wife, who has sacrificed so much over the past twenty-five years of our marriage and ministry.

In Loving Memory of Joseph F. Purpura Sr., my father, a man who was always an example of right living.

CHAPTER 1
INTRODUCTION

Young people today are confronted with moral and ethical choices at a younger age than in past decades. They are tempted to partake of illicit drugs, alcohol, and/or tobacco. They are confronted with choices of whether to participate in pre-marital sexual relations - heterosexual or homosexual or to abstain, whether to view pornography not only in secret but also on their family television or over the Internet connection from their own bedroom. These are among the many choices confronting young people today. Often they are confronting these issues as early as in their pre-teen years. The multitude of moral and ethical choices confronting pre-teens and teens often find these young people ill prepared to make responsible and educated choices. Children ought to be protected from such issues until they are old enough to deal with them maturely. The reality of our time, however, is that our society is so permeated with immoral/unethical behaviors that we as the Church, and as parents, must act to equip our children for responding in a meaningful and responsible way to all of these issues. This project will focus on the current moral and ethical issues confronting Orthodox Christian Youth. Attention will be given to the Church's teaching concerning these issues as well as to what we as Church, as parents, as people working with and concerned with youth can do to better equip our young people for making good choices and right decisions on pressing issues. It is not the intent of this project to deal with the crises of moral decay in society by rolling back the flood of questionable presentations of inappropriate material in the media, schools and society at large. It is this author's belief, however, that better equipping our young people to make healthy decisions will produce healthier communities.

In 1992 this author conducted a 142-question survey of teens in the Antiochian Orthodox Christian Archdiocese. Much was learned from that survey, and the data produced by it led to changes in the focus of Youth Ministry efforts in the Antiochian Orthodox Christian Archdiocese of North America. As a consequence, greater focus is now placed on meeting the needs of teens in addressing current issues confronting them in their daily life. This is done through Christ-centered ministry. This approach led teens to be more aware of the issues and to better articulate the teachings of the Church on many of the social issues contemporary to 1992. Hopefully these teens were able, as a result, to make better choices in their own lives.

Much seems to have changed since those days in early 1992. Most of the teens of the early 1990s have moved on and in many cases have completed college and are now starting their careers. As a youth director working with teens on a daily basis, the need for more current tools to assess the needs of contemporary teens has become apparent. The social moral and ethical agenda as a whole has changed since what now seem 'the quiet days of the early 1990s'. Television has drastically changed, showing adult oriented material at all hours of the day and even material that would have been unacceptable at any hour just ten years ago. The Internet has blossomed and has brought much good with it, but has also brought a whole new set of moral and ethical issues. The social agendas of many groups concerning moral and ethical behaviors once thought of as socially unacceptable have now become part of mainstream teaching in the schools and are protected by many state laws. The need to re-assess current teen life has become apparent. There is a need to measure whether we are dealing with the same issues, new ones, or a combination of new and old. We need to see what impact the major social changes of this decade are having on young people. Therefore, this author has embarked on a new, more expanded, survey of teens, particularly concerning moral and ethical issues. This new survey is identified in the remainder of this project as *The Orthodox Teen Survey*. This project will deal with why we need to make this assessment, why we need to be concerned with young people, what the issues are confronting them, what the Church[1] teaches and has taught on these issues throughout Her 2000 year history as well as what we can and ought to do in response.

One only has to casually read the newspapers or listen to the evening news to understand many of the issues confronting young people. Even if the issues are not new, they are certainly more public. Greater publicity advertises such behaviors to teens, perhaps making them more susceptible to participation in those behaviors. A quick scan of one major newspaper over a period of three months, gives a glimpse of the numerous issues young people face. A February 10, 1999 article in *The Boston Globe* read, "Survey finds half of TV shows refer to sex, few responsibly."[2] The article starts off by saying that sex is not exactly taboo on television, "but one subject seems to be largely off-limits, according to a major new study released yesterday: the 'risks and responsibilities' of sexual activity"[3] A survey conducted by the Henry J. Kaiser Family Foundation as reported in this news article reported that 67 percent of prime time shows contained sexual content in words or deeds. The article goes on:

> With teenage pregnancies reaching 1 million per year and sexually transmitted diseases annually striking more than 3 million teenagers, the sexual messages sent by TV are a matter of growing significance, according to Vicky Rideout, director of the foundation's program on the Entertainment Media and Public Health.
>
> "Surveys indicate that TV is one of the top sources of information for young people about sex," Rideout said in an interview. "Obviously parents and sex-ed classes in schools are important, but TV is a part of sexual socialization of young people. It shows how men and women relate to each other, and what the norms of sexual behavior are."
>
> Just in case anyone was still in doubt, the study makes clear just how preoccupied television has become with sex. Fully 85 percent of soap operas were found to contain sexual content; TV movies, 83 percent; talk shows, 78 percent; dramas, 58 percent; newsmagazines, 58 percent; sitcoms, 56 percent; reality shows, 23 percent.[4]

---

[1] "Church" in all cases throughout this project refers to the Orthodox Christian Church.

[2] Don Aucoin, "Survey Finds half of TV Shows refer to sex, few responsibly," *The Boston Globe,* 10 February 1999, A17.

[3] Ibid.

[4] Ibid.

In another article we read that teens are open to abstinence from sex on TV:

> Hit television shows are rife with sexual banter, kissing, and implied sex, yet they don't bother to channel messages about abstinence or safe sex[5] through their widely popular characters, says Bianca DuJour, 15, ... "The message is that sex is an everyday thing and everybody does it, because they are so casual about it" on television.
>
> The messages are even more important now with widespread sexual activity at younger ages, according to surveys, and increased HIV infection and other sexually transmitted diseases among younger people, said teen advocates.
>
> ... In interviews yesterday, teenagers in and around Boston said that the shows they love most would not lose popularity if producers decided to work in dialogue about safe sex, or abstinence.[6]

Sexual activity of teens appears to be on the rise, so also are the effects:

> The Kaiser Family Foundation reports - Of The 15 to 17 million new cases of STDs that will plague Americans this year, upwards of a quarter will afflict 15-to-19-year-olds, researchers report.
>
> While many factors figure in to the high STD rates, one of the most obvious is that most students have had sex by the time they graduate from high school—often, unprotected sex. For example:
>
> - More than one-third of ninth-graders and two-thirds of twelfth-graders have had intercourse.
> - One in three sexually active teenage girls opts for no contraception at all.
> - While use of the pill and other hormonal method of birth control are on the rise, they offer no protection against STDs.
> - Meanwhile, more teen-agers are turning to oral sex—not realizing that, while offering protection against HIV, oral transmission of other STDs is becoming increasing common.[7]

In addition to the issues of sexuality, we read and hear about the war on abortion. Things have become so skewed that people on the opposite sides of the issues use each other's points to argue their own. Those who are committed to preserving the life of the unborn child in some cases have resorted to clinic bombings[8] and other scare tactics, while those taking the life of the unborn fight for their own rights of safety and life. Just a few generations ago abortion was clearly seen as wrong by the majority of Americans, while

---

[5] The author does not intend to convey here that he is an advocate of "safe sex" as known today. The author strongly supports the teaching of the Church that the only "safe sex" is between married couples who were virgins prior to marriage and are faithful to one another in marriage. The author further has difficulty with the term of "safe sex" as used today because it implies that the methods are 100% safe, which they are not, and the term assumes that there is no emotional and spiritual "fall-out" from pre-marital or extramarital affairs, which there are consequences.

[6] Jordana Hart, "Teens open to safe sex, abstinence on TV," *The Boston Globe,* 10 February 1999, A16.

[7] The risks of young love, Jennifer Kornreich, MSNBC, March 20, 2001, http://www.msnbc.com

[8] Associated Press, "Agents say clinic bomber used remote," *The Boston Globe,* 30 January 1999, A5.

today our nation is divided on this issue and that division is reflected in the views of our teens on this issue.

Homosexuality, a behavior once unseen and unheard of by the vast majority of Americans and certainly our children (save child sexual abuse) is now out in the open, protected by many laws, taught in schools as an acceptable alternative lifestyle and actively pursued by some teens in Middle School, High School and Colleges, either as a way of life or "the thing to do." Efforts by some Southern Baptist churches to help gays "change" is seen as something new and patronizing[9], despite the existence of this issue in the life of the Church since Her earliest days. This issue rages on in our society with people on both sides of the issue fighting for their positions, and again our young people are affected by the fallout of these issues as reflected in the views, and behavior, of teens in *The Orthodox Teen Survey*.

Alcohol abuse, while not a new issue, has risen in prominence to the degree that, "Colleges declare war on drinking: two-dozen campuses adopt anti-alcohol pact."[10] Despite the fact that alcohol is better understood today as a drug that is a gateway to other drugs and "risk-taking behaviors," alcohol consumption appears to be on the rise in colleges, as well as amongst the teens in *The Orthodox Teen Survey*:

> The announcement comes as some studies show college alcohol consumption increasing and a little over a year after the highly publicized death of Scott Kruger, a Massachusetts Institute of Technology freshman who died after a night of heavy drinking at a fraternity. Nationwide last year, 34 students died on campuses after drinking heavily.
>
> A 1997 national survey shows there has been an increase in the frequency and consumption of alcohol by college students. According to the survey of students in 116 colleges and universities, some 52.3 percent of students say they drink to get drunk. In 1993, that figure was 39.4 percent.[11]

Further, the National Center on Addiction and Substance Abuse reports:

> "Alcohol is far and away the top drug of abuse for American kids," said Sue Foster, the director of policy research at the National Center on Addiction and Substance Abuse. "The college binge-drinking problem starts with children and teens, and that's where our prevention and education efforts must be focused."
>
> Califano said "underage drinking has reached epidemic proportions in America." The report, he added, "is a clarion call for national mobilization to curb underage drinking."
>
> The estimate of teens who binge drink—31 percent among high school students—was obtained by using the Youth Risk Behavior Survey of the federal Centers for Disease Control and Prevention in Atlanta, published in 2000. Binge drinking often is described as four consecutive drinks for a female or five drinks for a male.
>
> According to an American Medical Association survey last year, binge drinking is among parents' top worries. Around 44 percent of college students admit to binge drinking, and nearly a fourth of those do it frequently.
>
> The center, which is based at Columbia University in New York City, also cited these results from the Youth Risk Behavior Survey:
>
> •The gender gap for drinking is disappearing. Female ninth-graders were just as likely to be drinkers as male ninth-graders.

---

[9] Vicki Brown, Associated Press Writer, "Church to teach gays can 'change,'" *The Boston Globe* (date not available).
[10] Beth Daley, "Colleges declare war on drinking," *The Boston Globe,* 7 December1998, B1.
[11] Ibid

●Eighty-one percent of high school students have consumed alcohol, compared with 70 percent who have smoked cigarettes and 47 percent who have used marijuana.

●Most teens who experiment with alcohol continue using it. Among high school seniors who had tried alcohol, 91.3 percent still were drinking in the 12th grade.[12]

At the same time, "Colleges confront rising stress levels among students":

"Warning: Attending College can cause headaches, nausea, sleeplessness, irritation, and eating disorders."

... ...

But all those maladies are symptoms of stress, and all, according to campus officials and counselors, are being found in increasing numbers of students. They say more students are arriving at college barely able to cope when pressure builds.

"We are seeing today's college student having the problems that you might expect a 40-year-old executive to have, from stomach disorders to headaches," said Fred Newton, the director of counseling services at Kansas State University.

Experts point to numerous reasons for this generation's seeming more stressed, including the breakdown of the traditional family. Increasingly, students come from homes of divorce, or from homes where parents were so busy and stressed themselves that they had no time to talk out their children's problems.[13]

Further complicating the issues confronting our young people are the expanded capabilities of science. While the vast number of strides in science, medicine and technology has served people well, technology at times has outpaced our ability or desire to develop a coherent understanding of the implications of that technology and the appropriate use of it. While this is not new human history, the pace at which these new technologies arise is new. An example of this growth and need to better regulate and understand the implications can be found in the issues surrounding cloning. While cloning holds much hope for people in need of healthy organs, it also raises the fear of great abuses. The Orthodox Church of Greece expressed her concern over cloning with these words:

The head of the Orthodox Church in Greece is concerned that scientists trying to clone human beings may be stepping over the boundaries ordained by nature.

The archbishop of Athens and all Greece warned at a medical conference that cloning could result in the creation of a race of human copies, amounting to a nightmare worse than Frankenstein's monster.

... Warning that nature avenges itself against those who fail to respect it, the archbishop added: "This will create a race of human copies, just as Nazis and Soviets tried to do. Frankenstein and the Nazi genetics researcher Joseph Mengele would pale by comparison."

Christodoulos is worried that the moral understanding of those who wield the tools of science may be lacking, inadequate to the task of assessing what kind is wrong. He's concerned that the products of science may be misused to the detriment of humanity they were intended to serve.

Though he is sounding the alarm in the starkest of terms, Christodoulos acknowledges that genetic research has many benefits for mankind. His point is simply that there need to

---

[12] Statement by The National Center on Addiction and Substance, February 26, 2002, Ellen Ross, http://www.casacolumbia.org.

[13] Knight Ridder, "Colleges confront rising stress levels among students," *The Boston Globe,* 26 December1998, A9.

Why is it parents can explain the harmful
effects of one and not the other?

TEENS WHO SAY THEY HAVE LEARNED A LOT ABOUT THE RISKS OF MARIJUANA FROM

THEIR PARENTS ARE 40% LESS LIKELY TO USE POT AS THOSE TEENS WHO SAY THEY

HAVE LEARNED NOTHING ABOUT DRUGS FROM THEIR PARENTS. TALK TO YOUR CHILD

ABOUT MARIJUANA. KNOWLEDGE IS PRETTY CONTAGIOUS STUFF. IF YOU NEED HELP,

VISIT OUR WEB SITES AT www.projectknow.com or www.drugfreeamerica.org.

CALL 1-800-788-2800 FOR A FREE COPY OF "MARIJUANA: FACTS PARENTS NEED TO KNOW."

**Office of National Drug Control Policy
Partnership for a Drug-Free America**

be stricter controls on it, that man's power over nature needs to be regulated by sound moral and ethical judgment.[14]

It is on issues such as cloning that the Church Herself needs to better articulate Her teaching, so as to enable our current and future scientists and young people to better understand the choices before them. It is this same ability to discern that needs to be imparted to our young people who are often mesmerized by the rapid changes and developments of technology. This becomes particularly important as what mesmerizes them today may well be the technology that they and their children use in the future as an everyday event.

Perhaps the most tragic of all issues, is the lack of good moral and ethical models for our young people to emulate. So much has been attached to "being successful" as the bottom line; we have robbed young people of the joy of living life, and living life well, in a healthy and complete way. Few role models of "good" moral and ethical people are held in high esteem in the news and general media. The bottom line of how much money, power or fame one has, despite their lifestyle, has been the overriding measure of success presented to young people.

The office of National Drug Control Policy sums the issues of drugs and perhaps several of the issues above, up well with a one page ad in the February 1, 1999 issues of U.S. News and World Report" as shown above. [15]

The point here is not to criticize parents or teens, but to recognize the need to work with both and to better equip both parents and teens to deal with the issues confronting teens, parents and families. In another large ad in the Boston Globe, the Office of National Drug Control Policy reminds the reader of resources available to children, teens, and parents. The caption below a picture of a grandfather listening to his grandson reads, "The Power of Grandpa." The ad goes on to say:

---

[14] "Church of Greece Concerned Over Cloning," *The Orthodox Observer,* 20 November 1998, 20.

[15] Ad appeared in issue of *U.S. News and World Report,* February 1, 1999.

Children have a very special relationship with Grandma and Grandpa. That's why grandparents can be such powerful allies in helping keep a kid off drugs.

Grandparents are cool, relaxed, they're not on the firing line every day. Some days a kid hates his folks. He never hates his grandparents. Grandparents ask direct, point-blank, embarrassing questions you're too nervous to ask:

"Who's the girl?"
"How come you're doing poorly in history?"
"Why are your eyes always red?"
"Did you go to the doctor? What did he say?"

The same kid who cons his parents is ashamed to lie to Grandpa. Without betraying their trust, a loving, understanding grandparent can discuss the danger of drugs openly with the child he adores. And he should.[16]

One of the goals of this project is to help identify some of the sources that youth workers, parents, clergy, teens, and concerned adults can utilize in better equipping young people to deal with the day to day issues confronting them in life. Certainly grandparents and other senior adults in our communities are one of those resources. This resource amongst others will be explored in later chapters keeping in mind the words of Metropolitan Theodosius[17]:

The ultimate mission statement is drafted by our actions, not our words. It demands that we "strive for excellence" not as an ideological imperative, but as a sign of God's presence in our lives. It challenges us to be loving as Christ is loving, to suffer as Christ suffers, to rejoice in the least of the brethren as Christ rejoices, and finally, to share in Christ's victory over sin and death. Jesus Christ comes into the world to act; He is the One in Whom we place our faith and the One from Whom we learn to proclaim our faith through our actions and lives.[18]

The next chapter explores the importance of young people's moral and ethical development in light of the Scriptures. Every Ministry needs to start with God, with what He sees as important and right in order to understand what are good choices in one's life. Enabling young people to make good choices is important in that they can deliberately change themselves and the world around them. It is with the understanding that the newspaper articles quoted earlier need not be the norm for our young people that this author explores the scriptures and presents the remainder of this project. The next chapter will also explore what God expects of those who are called to minister amongst young people, particularly since adults can and do have a profound impact on the young people to whom they minister, interact and simply set the standards for right behavior through their own actions.

The third chapter will turn to the teens themselves. In order to bring our young people to Christ and develop a meaningful relationship between them, Jesus Christ and His Church, it

---

[16] Ad for the Office of National Drug Control Policy: Partnership for a Drug-Free New England and America, *The Boston Globe,* 26 January 1999, A9.

[17] Metropolitan Theodosius is the Archbishop of Washington and Metropolitan of All North America and Canada of the Orthodox Church in America.

[18] Metropolitan Theodosius, "1998 Nativity Message of His Beatitude, Metropolitan Theodosius," *The Orthodox Church,* December 1998, 1.

is essential to understand the teens themselves—who they are, what they believe, what they like, what they fear and what they do. This author firmly believes that in understanding the issues confronting teens, as well as addressing those issues in dialogue and exploration with teens, teens can come to a much deeper understanding of Christ, and develop a deeper more meaningful relationship with Him. It is also believed that by addressing the issues confronting teens one can teach the scriptures, theology, and worship life of the Church and present them in a life changing manner to young people in a way that will have impact and meaning.

The final chapter will explore a few of the major issues identified in the survey. While only a few of the issues will be explored it is hoped that the reader will be able to view these as an example of how one might address these and the many other issues raised in the survey. Being able to address the issues in light of Christ is essential in that the goal of this project is to identify the issues so that one can better minister to teens. Ministering to teens means being able to move them from where they are into a deeper relationship with Christ and to help them live their lives as though that relationship really matters.

CHAPTER 2
THE IMPORTANCE OF YOUTH AND THEIR MORAL AND ETHICAL DEVELOPMENT IN LIGHT OF THE SCRIPTURES

Aside from dealing with the struggles of rapid changes during adolescence, young people are called to bear witness to Christ to those younger than they, their peers, and even to their elders. This section briefly provides for understanding the importance of young people in the scriptures. It surveys the Scriptural and Patristic expectations of behavior placed upon those who are called to be an example to the young, as well as the expectations of the young themselves who have been called by God to be His children. This chapter will lay the groundwork as to why the Church, Parents, Pastors, Teachers, Youth Workers and others, as well as young people themselves, need be concerned with what is right and wrong. This concern needs to lead to teaching and "handing down" that teaching and way of life.

"Train up a child in the way he should go, and when he is old he will not depart from it." (Proverbs 22:6)[19] This verse from scripture in many ways guided the author in the writing of this work. Likewise, the words of our Lord and Savior Jesus Christ as recorded in Matthew 18:5-7, concerning children was much in the mind of this author.

> "Whoever receives one such child in my name receives me; but whoever causes one of these little ones who believe in me to sin, it would be better for him to have a great millstone fastened round his neck and to be drowned in the depth of the sea.
> "Woe to the world for temptations to sin! For it is necessary that temptations come, but woe to the man by whom the temptation comes!" (*Matthew 18:5-7*)

The Biblical texts of Jeremiah and Paul's letter to Timothy stand out as reminders to us of the significant impact and place that young people can and do have in the life of the Church.

> Command and teach these things. Let no one despise your youth, but set the believers an example in speech and conduct, in love, in faith, in purity. Till I come, attend to the public reading of scripture, to preaching, to teaching. Do not neglect the gift you have, which was given you by prophetic utterance when the council of elders laid their hands upon you. Practice these duties, devote yourself to them, so that all may see your progress. Take heed to yourself and to your teaching; hold to that, for by so doing you will save both yourself and your hearers. (*1 Timothy 4:11-16*)

St. John Chrysostom in his homily on Timothy recognizes that young people can attain great spiritual and leadership heights, as did Timothy, even in his youth:

---

[19] All scriptural quotes are taken from the Revised Standard Version, unless otherwise noted since this is the Biblical text used in most Orthodox Churches in North America.

> For so preeminent in virtue was Timothy, that his youth was no impediment to his promotion; therefore he writes, "Let no man despise thy youth" (1 Tim. iv. 12, and v. 2); and again, "The younger women as sisters." For where there is virtue, all other things are superfluous, and there can be no impediment.[20]

A similar reference is made of Jeremiah:

> ... but the LORD said to me, "Do not say, 'I am only a youth'; for to all to whom I send you you shall go, and whatever I command you you shall speak. Be not afraid of them, for I am with you to deliver you, says the LORD." *(Jeremiah 1:7-8)*

Texts from the Apostles and St. Basil concerning youth have also influenced this writer. St. Basil recognizes the time of childhood and youth as the time for change and learning, as recorded in these two passages:

> What clearer proof of our faith could there be than that we were brought up by our grandmother, a blessed woman, who came from among you? I have reference to the illustrious Macrina, by whom we were taught the words of the most blessed Gregory, which, having been preserved until her time by uninterrupted tradition, she also guarded, and she formed and molded me, still a child, to the doctrines of piety. But, after we received the power of understanding, and reason had been perfected in us through age, having traversed much of the earth and sea, whenever we found any who were walking according to the traditional rule of piety, we claimed them as our fathers and made them the guides of our soul on the journey to God.[21]
>
> The prescribed time for a child who is capable of learning is until youth. The youth, having attained to his twenty-first year, when he begins to cover his cheeks with the first growth of beard, imperceptibly disappears, since the adolescent has already changed into the man. Accordingly, when you see a man who has laid aside the progressive increase according to age, who is already advanced in his reasoning, and who bears no trace of youth, will you not think that the past has died in him? Again, the old man, transposed into another form and another disposition of soul, is evidently another man, as compared with the former. So that the life of men is wont to be fulfilled through many deaths, not only by the change in the passing from one age to another, but also by the lapses of the souls through sin.[22]

The apostles write in the Didache: "Do not take your hand from your son or your daughter, but teach them the fear of God from their youth."[23]

Many examples abound of young people who strove to live upright lives, even despite their surroundings. An example is St. Honoratus as described in a sermon by St. Hilary:

> My sermon rather hastens on to this aspect of his life: the faith with which, in the years of his youth, by his own free choice he desired baptism; the mature wisdom which he showed in fearing death, though in good health; how he clearly discerned that without

---

[20] John Chrysostom, "The Homilies of St. John Chrysostom, Archbishop of Constantinople, On the Epistles of St. Paul the Apostle to Timothy, Titus, and Philemon. Argument 1 on Timothy," Patristic Reference Library Volume 1. Nicene and Post Nicene Fathers—Volume 13, reproduced in *FaithWorx* [CD-Rom] (Theologic Systems Electronic Reference Library, http://www.theologic.com, Version 2.0, 1998).

[21] St. Basil. Fathers of the Church—Volume 28—Letters - 204. to the Neo-Caesareans 1:16, reproduced in *FaithWorx* [CD-Rom] (Theologic Systems Electronic Reference Library, http://www.theologic.com, Version 2.0, 1998).

[22] St. Basil. Fathers of the Church—Volume 46—Exegetic Homilies—Homily 22:5 On Psalm 114, reproduced in *FaithWorx* [CD-Rom] (Theologic Systems Electronic Reference Library, http://www.theologic.com, Version 2.0, 1998).

[23] FaithWorx Patristic Reference Library Volume 3. Fathers of the Church—Volume 1. The Didache or Teaching of the Twelve Apostles. Chapter 4:6

baptism he would be without life; how he thirsted and yearned for the renewal of his life; how sweet was infancy to him; how modest his boyhood; how serious his youth; how he surpassed all, even of every age, in grace and virtue, and was always found older than himself, so that you would think truly that he had been trained in some heavenly school. He was instructed without any urging on the part of his family. With God's help, he persevered in his desire of baptism without being importuned by men; and, what is greater than all this, while his baptismal splendor was still fresh and unmarred, with no one to urge him, he embraced the monastic life.[24]

Importance of Children in the Bible

We know that in the Old Testament it was God's promise of children and their descendants that stood at the heart of the Covenant. Abraham, despite all that God had given him, still felt at a great loss as he was childless and had no heir.

> After these things the word of the LORD came to Abram in a vision, "Fear not, Abram, I am your shield; your reward shall be very great." But Abram said, "O Lord GOD, what wilt thou give me, for I continue childless, and the heir of my house is Eliezer of Damascus?" And Abram said, "Behold, thou hast given me no offspring; and a slave born in my house will be my heir." And behold, the word of the LORD came to him, "This man shall not be your heir; your own son shall be your heir." And he brought him outside and said, "Look toward heaven, and number the stars, if you are able to number them." Then he said to him, "So shall your descendants be." And he believed the LORD; and he reckoned it to him as righteousness. *(Genesis 15:1 - 15:6)*

The Scriptures are filled with references to children and young people. Children throughout the scriptures are seen as a gift from God who are expected to be nurtured and cared for, as well as to be raised from the earliest of age conscious of God and the traditions of the family and people of God. The Old Testament regarded children in the family as a mark of divine favor and needed for marital and family fulfillment (Gen. 15:2; 30:1; 1 S. 1:11, 20; Ps. 127:3; Lk. 1:7, 28).

The Book of Psalms beautifully presents the image of the family.

> Your wife will be like a fruitful vine within your house; your children will be like olive shoots around your table. Lo, thus shall the man be blessed who fears the LORD. *(Psalms 128:3 - 128:4)*

This same Psalm is sung in the Orthodox Marriage Service as the Priest leads the married couple around the table where the marriage service takes place, emphasizing the Church's view of importance of children within the context of marriage. We know that from the very beginning of man and woman's relationship with God, children played an important role in the continuation of the creation of the world and the relationship with God. Children in the Old Testament were seen as a way of living on for the parents. Children were also seen as possessions of their parents with no rights and status in society.

---

[24] Roy J. Deferrari, Ph.D, trans., "A Sermon On The Life Of St. Honoratus By St. Hilary," *Fathers of the Church—Volume 15.* A Sermon on the Life of St. Honoratus, Chapter 1:5, reproduced in *FaithWorx* [CD-Rom] (Theologic Systems Electronic Reference Library, http://www.theologic.com, Version 2.0, 1998).

In the New Testament, children likewise are important with one major change. Jesus radically alters the status quo and place of children within the community.

> Hans-Rudi Weber, in his World Council of Churches study "Jesus and the Children," written to honor the International Year of the Child in 1979, says that Jesus' attitude to children was so new and astonishing that one wonders whether the Christian church since then has fully understood these amazing actions and sayings.[25]

If in fact Jesus' actions and teaching concerning children were radically different, then we, as youth workers and Christian leaders, must understand that radical change. We will look at Christ's words and interaction with children in the Gospels, as well as those of the writers of the epistles and the great Church leaders and teachers who have followed them, in order to better understand this radical change. It is precisely with this message and with what it means for our own life and interaction with young people that the remainder of this chapter will concern itself.

St. Mark, in his gospel, presents children as models of discipleship, as can be seen in the events involving Jesus, his disciples, and children. There was a direct public confrontation with the disciples, who were thinking and acting as though children should not bother the Master or be in his presence. (Mark 10:13—16). St. John Chrysostom says the disciples prevented the children from coming to Christ, "For dignity"[26] or one can say for *power or pride*. St. John goes on to write in reference to Jesus' words,

> Let us also then, if we would be inheritors of the Heavens, possess ourselves of this virtue with much diligence. For this is the limit of true wisdom; to be simple with understanding; this is angelic life; yes, for the soul of a little child is pure from all the passions… Therefore He said, "of such is the kingdom of Heaven," that by choice we should practice these things, which young children have by nature.[27]

The following event clearly states the place infants, children, and young people ought to have in the Church today. Just as Jesus accepted them, so ought we. In Mark 10:13-16 we see Jesus' response,

> And they were bringing children to him that he might touch them; and the disciples rebuked them. [14]But when Jesus saw it he was indignant, and said to them, "Let the children come to me, do not hinder them; for to such belongs the kingdom of God. [15]Truly, I say to you, whoever does not receive the kingdom of God like a child shall not enter it." [16]And he took them in his arms and blessed them, laying his hands upon them. *(Mark 10:13 - 16)*

This very action of Jesus taking the children up into his arms and blessing them, is a clear sign of His love and acceptance of children, and even more so of their place among the followers of Christ. In fact this very embrace of the child by Jesus is thought by some to be the very sign of the messianic coming.

---

[25] Lynlea Rodger, "The Infancy Stories of Matthew and Luke," *Horizons in Biblical Theology,* June 1997. (Pittsburgh, Pittsburgh Theological Seminary), 62.

[26] St. John Chrysostom, "Homilies on St. Matthew," *The Nicene and Post Nicene Fathers*, Volume X, (Grand Rapids, WM B. Eerdmans Publishing Company1975), 385.

[27] Ibid.

It was in fact a messianic embrace, an echo of Luke 2:28, when Simeon took the child Jesus in his arms. It is the embrace of the father who welcomes the return of the son who was lost (16:20). According to a rabbinic treatise, the resurrection of the people of Israel will occur when "God embraces them, presses them to his heart, and kisses them, thus bringing them into the life of the world to come" (Seder Bijahu Rabba 17). Hence the embrace of Jesus is also the embrace of the Messianic King.[28]

Matthew 19:13-15, records this messianic embrace as we see Jesus welcoming the little children,

> Then children were brought to him that he might lay his hands on them and pray. The disciples rebuked the people; but Jesus said, "Let the children come to me, and do not hinder them; for to such belongs the kingdom of heaven." And he laid his hands on them and went away. (*Matthew 19:13—15*)

Again, Luke records this embrace as we see an even stronger rendition of these words,

> Now they were bringing even infants to him that he might touch them; and when the disciples saw it, they rebuked them. But Jesus called them to him, saying, "Let the children come to me, and do not hinder them; for to such belongs the kingdom of God. Truly, I say to you, whoever does not receive the kingdom of God like a child shall not enter it." *(Luke 18:15—17)*

Jesus, by telling His disciples to let the children come to him, and even more so by His blessing them, states that children are blessed, that they belong to the Kingdom of God here and now, and not just at some future point. So often, we refer to our young people as "the future of the Church." Young people often equate this as our saying they are not presently part of the church in any real or meaningful way—yet our Lord says that they are important now and members of the Kingdom of heaven here and now on earth.

This same presence and blessing is the rationale used in the Orthodox Church for saying that marriage is blessed because of Christ's presence at the marriage feast in Cana of Galilee and the miracle He performed there, "O Lord our God, who in thy saving providence didst vouchsafe by thy presence in Cana of Galilee to declare marriage honorable."[29] It is Christ's calling the children to Him, His presence amongst them, His blessing them, and His statement, "to such as these that the kingdom of God belongs," that rightfully establishes the place of children in the Church. It is important to note that all three synoptic Gospels thought this event was important enough that they all recorded it, almost identically. Furthermore, the practice from antiquity of chrismating children into full membership into the Church and at the same time their partaking of the Body and Blood of Christ, even from infancy, sets the child as a full sacramental member of the Church. This partaking of the body and blood of Christ in Holy Communion sets the child as a member of the Kingdom of God here and now on earth, "He who eats my flesh and drinks my blood abides in me, and I in him." (*John 6:56*)

---

[28] Rodger, "The Infancy Stories of Matthew and Luke," 76.

[29] Service Book of the Holy Eastern Orthodox Catholic and Apostolic Church: according to the use of the Antiochian Orthodox Christian Archdiocese of North America. (Englewood, New Jersey: Antiochian Orthodox Christian Archdiocese, 1971), 178.

Jesus takes His acceptance of children further by placing them in a position of prominence and stating, "Whoever causes one of these little ones who believe in me to sin, it would be better for him if a great millstone were hung round his neck and he were thrown into the sea." (*Mark 9:42*) Again, in Luke he states, "It would be better for him if a millstone were hung round his neck and he were cast into the sea, than that he should cause one of these little ones to sin." (*Luke 17:2*) Likewise, in Matthew, "So it is not the will of my Father who is in heaven that one of these little ones should perish." (*Matthew 18:14*) As a reminder that children are protected by God, Jesus states, "See that you do not despise one of these little ones; for I tell you that in heaven their angels always behold the face of my Father who is in heaven." (*Matthew 18:10*) Moreover, Matthew reminds us how precious children are to God, "And whoever gives to one of these little ones[30] even a cup of cold water because he is a disciple, truly, I say to you, he shall not lose his reward."

(*Matthew 10:42*) Jesus uses of the word "truly" here and in the passage of Luke where he says, "Truly, I say to you, whoever does not receive the kingdom of God like a child shall not enter it" *(Luke 18:17)* to emphasize to the reader that what He is about to say after the word "truly" is important and He wants the listener to pay special attention. In this case He stresses the importance of children and the radically different place in society to which he places them. In both the Hebrew Old Testament and Greek philosophical world, while children were seen as a blessing, they still had no status and were viewed as property of their parents. Rodger saw Jesus changing the status quo of children:

> This means that Jesus is subverting through the metaphor of the child the conventional understanding of the law as the route to the Kingdom, and the association for Jews of the Kingdom of God with the reciting of the Shema. It was held that a child could receive the Kingdom only if he obediently learned to pray the Shema and learned Torah on which it was based. If this interpretation is accepted, Jesus was on this occasion challenging the Rabbinic understanding of how the Kingdom of Heaven is to be received, and set the metaphor of the child in the place of the liturgical practice of reciting the Shema. Importantly also, the child is intended to be understood in a generic context, and is not gender specific. This tradition about Jesus, which is recorded by all Synoptics, but placed in different contexts in their accounts, calls a halt to the disciples who are reported as spending much time on the question of who is the greatest in the Kingdom of heaven. In this narration of the blessing of children by Jesus, Jesus' action is congruent with the record in Luke 9:46 where Jesus places a child at his side, i.e. in the place of authority and as the response to the disciples' questions. It is an image of divine hospitality, consistent with Jesus' practice of a radical table fellowship and a Kingdom which challenged all forms of cultural and religious brokerage. That the envoy and representatives of Jesus, and through him God, could be a child was a shocking thing, and as incomprehensible to the disciples as that the Messiah had to suffer. Variations of the teaching about the first and the last is a significant theme in the Synoptics, and is frequently specifically referenced to children."[31]

---

[30] The writer understands that in Matthew this may refer to more than just the physical age of a person, though the author includes it here, because of its relevance to caring for those of "less powerful status" than the one the words are intended for.

[31] Rodger, "The Infancy Stories of Matthew and Luke," 76-77.

"Children and youngsters play a distinct role in Mark's dramatic sequence. Jesus' greatest miracle is the raising of the twelve-year-old daughter of Jairus (5:35-43)."[32] It is the raising of this little girl that tells us who Jesus is in all His power and glory,

> Now when John heard in prison about the deeds of the Christ, he sent word by his disciples and said to him, "Are you he who is to come, or shall we look for another?" And Jesus answered them, "Go and tell John what you hear and see: the blind receive their sight and the lame walk, lepers are cleansed and the deaf hear, and the dead are raised up, and the poor have good news preached to them. (*Matthew11:2-5*)

We read in the Gospel of Mark other accounts of miracles that include young people; the boy afflicted with an illness resembling epilepsy (Mark 9:14-29). It is a young man in the passion account who closely follows Jesus after the disciples have fled (Mark 14:50-51). When Mary Magdalene and the other woman approach the tomb of Christ, wondering how they will roll away the stone from the entrance, they are "amazed" to see the tomb open, Jesus body not there and a young man sitting there.[33]

In Matthew, Jesus responds to the chief priests' indignation at the children calling Him "Hosanna" and the "son of David" during His entrance into Jerusalem by stating, "Yes; have you never read, 'Out of the mouth of babes and sucklings thou hast brought perfect praise'?" (*Matthew 21:16*) In response to the chief priests Jesus is referring to the Book of Isaiah when he says, "And as for me, this is my covenant with them, says the LORD: my spirit which is upon you, and my word which I have put in your mouth, shall not depart out of your mouth, or out of the mouth of your children, or out of the mouth of your children's children, says the LORD, from this time forth and for evermore."

(*Isaiah 59:21*). We see Jesus placing children in prominence and we hear him stating that God has prepared children to praise Him, which stands as another reminder to us as to the place of children in worship.

The child also becomes a model of right living in the Gospel of Matthew according to Lynlea Rodger who writes concerning the place of the child in the Gospel of Matthew:

> In his teaching the figure of the child is prominent. It is in love for enemies that we may be sons of God (5:45), a God who knows so intimately how to give good things to his children (7:7-13). Healings are offered as a release to those who in the care of God are his children (e.g. paralytic of 9:2, woman of 9:22). The wisdom of God is paradoxical, hidden from the wise and revealed to children (11:25), whose marketplace games are a parable of the condemnation of the Jewish sense of self sufficiency which did not recognize the call of God when it came upon them (10:16-17). It is the children who are free (17:24) and whose food scraps will become the feast of the Gentiles (15:21-8). There is no greater penalty than to the one who places a stumbling block before children (18:6-7), for the one who welcomes a child welcomes God Godself [Himself] (10:42, 18:1-5). Jesus took children in his arms, beckoned them (19:13-15), laid hands on them in blessing, healed children and drew on the image of the child to his followers as a sign of what was to be their own character and way relating (20:20-8), placing a child in their midst as a metaphor of discipleship (18:3). Jesus quotes scripture that it is out of the mouths of babes that God has prepared praise, and it is children in Matthew who cry out in Messianic acknowledgement in Jerusalem at what is to be the end of his life (21:15-16).[34]

---

[32] *The Anchor Bible Dictionary* 1992 ed., s.v. "Child, Children*"*
[33] Ibid.
[34] Rodger, "The Infancy Stories of Matthew and Luke," 73-75.

There are many other references in the scriptures attesting to the importance of and important roles children and young people have played in the history of Salvation. To name a few: God grants Joseph the gift of interpreting Pharaoh's dreams and ruling over the land of Egypt (Genesis 41:14-41). Samuel, who was called as a child, through the instruction of God, chooses David "the little one" above his older brothers (1 Sam 16:1-13). He allows David, so young and small that even Saul questions the thought of him going into battle, to slay the Philistine champion Goliath (I Sam 17:4-51). The children welcome Jesus into Jerusalem and shout Hosanna.

Moral and Ethical Aspects

Right living is essential in fulfilling Christ's command to bring the children to him. As parents, youth workers, clergy, parish leaders, young people, and members of the Christian Community, we are called to set the right example and do the right things in order to bring these children to Christ and keep them integrated in the life of the Church. The following pages are concerned with coming to an understanding of the scriptural understanding of right and wrong behavior, or right moral and ethical teaching and living.

> Biblical ethics is inalienably religious. Reflection on issues of moral conduct and character in scripture is always qualified by religious convictions and commitments. To abstract biblical ethics from its religious context is to distort it.[35]

It is precisely in this context of Jesus Christ, His Incarnation, His death, His Resurrection, and our desire to be His disciples, that Christian Ethics and Morals find their meaning and focus. It is by believing in Jesus Christ, as the Divine Logos, Incarnated in the flesh—His Resurrection from the dead and God dwelling amongst all people that suddenly the radically different moral and ethical values imparted to Christians from Christ make sense. The Evangelist John writes, "In the beginning was the Word, and the Word was with God, and the Word was God." (*John 1:1*). It is this same Word or Divine Logos, Jesus Himself who taught us to love even our enemies, to turn our cheek, to seek first the Kingdom of Heaven, to speak to women in public and to receive children in His Name. It is no longer enough to simply fulfill the law, but rather we are compelled to fulfill the law in spirit and in relationship with Christ. Being free from the law does not mean the law has been abolished, but rather that we have been called to live beyond (not *above*) the law. Living in relationship with the one and true God and seeking to be in relationship with Him, He becomes the focus and the rule of what is right and what is wrong. We seek to live a life that is well pleasing to God. This is to bring us beyond the law in such a way that we are not limited to the letter of law in doing only the good that the law prescribes as the minimum, or as a slave to the law. What is right should now be understood in ones heart and mind, for being in the presence of the Living God, allows one to see truth, and love, and at the same time to put the other (person) above our own needs.

---

[35] Allen D. Verhi, "Ethical Lists", *The Oxford Companion to the Bible.* Ed. Bruce M. Metzger. (New York, Oxford University Press1993), 202.

Freedom from the Law is not license to do as one pleases; rather it marks a new disposition created by the advent of the new age, a disposition marked by new powers of moral discernment and new possibilities of loving one's neighbor. Hence one does not need a law to identify the "works of the flesh" (Gal 5:19-21) or the "fruit of the Spirit" (Gal 5:22-23). Love sets one free and makes one capable of love; freedom fulfills itself in love; love constitutes the fulfillment of the whole Law (Gal 5:1-15). The indicative (you are free from the Law!) is bound inextricably to the imperative (love your neighbor as yourself!).[36]

God became a human being so that, "to all who received him, who believed in his name, he gave power to become children of God;" (*John 1:12*) Jesus came to reconcile us with God. He came to heal us and destroy that which separates us from God. Jesus makes it possible for us to live as brothers, sisters, and children of God, but this demands that we be led by the Spirit and put aside the desires of the flesh.[37]

This is the basis upon which stands Christian ethics as found in the New Testament. It is no longer a matter of following the letter of the law, but of living a life that allows us to accept God's gift of love and adoption as sons and daughters and by living our life in Christ, through the Holy Spirit. Jesus teaching and the sending of the Holy Spirit change the human condition.

Jesus of Nazareth came announcing that the kingdom of God was at hand and already making its power felt in his words and deeds. He called the people to repent, to form their conduct and character in response to the good news of that coming future. To welcome a future where the last will be first (Mark 10.31), a future already prefigured in Jesus' humble service, is to be ready to be "servant of all" (Mark 9.35). To delight in a kingdom where the poor will be blessed is now to be carefree about riches and to give alms. To repent before a kingdom that belongs to children, that is already prefigured in table fellowship with sinners, and that is signaled in open conversation with women, is to turn from conventional standards to bless children, welcome sinners, and treat women as equals. Because Jesus announced and already unveiled the coming reign of God, he spoke with authority, not simply on the basis of law and tradition. And because the coming reign of God demanded a response of the whole person and not merely external observance of the Law, his words made radical demands. So Jesus' radical demand for truthfulness replaced (and fulfilled) legal casuistry about oaths. The readiness to forgive and be reconciled set aside (and fulfilled) legal limitations on revenge. The disposition to love even enemies put aside legal debates about the meaning of neighbor. The ethics was based neither on the precepts of law nor the regularities of experience, nor did it discard them; law and wisdom were both qualified and fulfilled in this ethic of response to the future reign of the one God of scripture. Jesus died on a Roman cross, but his followers proclaimed that God had raised him up in an act of power that was at once his vindication and the prelude to God's final triumph. Moral reflection in the New Testament always looks back to the vindicated Jesus and forward to God's cosmic sovereignty.[38]

The ethical perspectives of the Early Church were shaped by the traditions of what Jesus did during His earthly ministry and by the church's experience of the Resurrection. The

---

[36] John C. Shelley, "Ethics in the New Testament." *Mercer Dictionary of the Bible*, (Macon, Georgia, Mercer University Press1990), 266.

[37] Chrysostom, "Homilies on the Epistle to the Romans: Homily XIV: Rom. Viii. 12,13," Translated by Rev. J. B. Morris, M.A., of Exeter College Oxford and Rev. W.H. Simcox Fellow of Queens College, Oxford, Revised, with notes, by George B. Stevens, PH.D. D.D., Professor in Yale University. reproduced in *FaithWorx* [CD-Rom] (Theologic Systems Electronic Reference Library, http://www.theologic.com, Version 2.0, 1998).

[38] Verhi, Ethical Lists, The Oxford Companion to the Bible, 204.

Resurrection, as St. Paul clearly states[39], stands at the very heart of why one is a Christian. The Resurrection for the Church was not simply a promise for our resurrection at the end of our earthly life, but rather an event, which radically changes who and what we are, as well as how we relate to one another and to God. Without the Resurrection, we cannot call God "our Father." It is precisely with this understanding that we can speak of Christian ethics, since we are no longer servants but children of God.

John Shelly makes several important points about the meaning of ethics in the New Testament. He states that ethics is the study of morals. It strives to present the moral perspectives of a particular group. In doing so it assumes that some behaviors are right while others are wrong. That certain qualities in a person are virtues, while others may be vices. That within a society certain behaviors are acceptable and good and others are bad and detrimental to the individual and the community at large. In short ethics answers the question of what a person ought to do, what they should strive to be like and how society should be organized. In the case of this project we are looking at,

> 'What ought I to do?' 'What kind of person ought I to be?' 'How ought society to be organized?' Our concern here is to describe the moral perspectives of the NT [New Testament], while remembering that for Christians these are also normative claims that prescribe how ought one to live.[40]

The Church, while she calls us to be perfect as God is perfect, understands that we are fallen and live in a fallen world. It is with this understanding of one's own *falleness* that this writer approaches the issues of right moral and ethical teaching. Not in the sense that it is right, good, or desirous to be in such a state, but that one must approach the subject with humility and understanding of one's own flaws rather than in a self-righteous manner. Most importantly this is not about who is better than another, but about life and death. This writer is motivated out of a sense and desire to move our young people to live and have life that comes from Christ alone. This writer well understands the struggles and temptations of this world, not out of pride but out of spiritual battle and one's own wounds. What the writer desires for youth is that they understand that this is about *spiritual warfare* and is a matter of spiritual life and death and in some cases even physical life and death. That while all people have moments in their lives that they are not proud of, what is important is that one change and turn to God, seeking His forgiveness and healing. St. John Chrysostom in his "Exhortation to Theodore after his fall," states this need clearly,

> Wherefore we have need of zeal in every direction, and much preparation of mind: and if we so order our conscience as to hate our former wickedness, and choose the contrary path with as much energy as God desires and commands, we shall not have anything less on account of the short space of time: many at least who were last have far outstripped those who were first. For to have fallen is not a grievous thing, but to remain prostrate after falling, and not to get up again; and, playing the coward and the sluggard, to conceal feebleness of moral purpose under the reasoning of despair. To whom also the prophet spoke in perplexity saying "Doth he who falleth not rise up, or he who turneth away not turn back?"[41]

---

[39] I Corinthians 15:12-18

[40] Shelley, "Ethics in the New Testament", *Mercer Dictionary of the Bible*, 265.

[41] John Chrysostom, "An Exhortation to Theodore After His Fall," Letter 1:7, *Nicene and Post-Nicene Fathers— Volume 9*, Translation, Rev. W.R.W. Stephens, M.A., reproduced in *FaithWorx* [CD-Rom] (Theologic Systems Electronic Reference Library, http://www.theologic.com, Version 2.0, 1998).

We want our young people to understand the need to struggle, to discern, to seek God's help, healing and restoration and ultimately to overcome their own failing, through Jesus Christ. We want our youth to understand, despite their failings and imperfections no matter what they are, God loves them and desires that they turn and be one with Him.

It is important to recognize that while the world has its measure of beauty and desire, the Church has a different measure of beauty. It is the Church's measure of beauty which talks of the person precisely as person and not as an object that needs to be understood and pursued by all in the Christian Community. Many young people have been driven by society to think that beauty is measured by outward physical appearance as defined by Madison Avenue. Pursuing outward beauty as an end in itself never allows people to know one another for who they really are and for what they have striven to become in their life. St. John Chrysostom distinguishes between physical and spiritual beauty,

> There is soul and body: they are two substances: there is a beauty of body, and there is a beauty of soul. What is beauty of body? An extended eyebrow, a merry glance, a blushing cheek, ruddy lips, a straight neck, long wavy hair, tapering fingers, upright stature, a fair blooming complexion. Does this bodily beauty come from nature, or from choice? Confessedly it comes from nature. ... Well! thou hast seen corporeal beauty.
>
> Now let us turn inward to the soul: ... Let us turn I say to the soul. Look upon that beauty, or rather listen to it: for thou canst not see it since it is invisible - Listen to that beauty. What then is beauty of soul? Temperance, mildness, almsgiving, love, brotherly kindness, tender affection, obedience to God, the fulfillment of the law, righteousness, contrition of heart. These things are the beauty of the soul. These things then are not the results of nature, but of moral disposition. And he who does not possess these things is able to receive them, and he who has them, if he becomes careless, loses them. For as in the case of the body I was saying that she who is ungraceful cannot become graceful; so in the case of the soul I say the contrary that the graceless soul can become full of grace... Seest thou that thou canst not alter grace of body, for it is the result not of moral disposition, but of nature. But grace of soul is supplied out of our own moral choice.[42]

We want our young people to understand and seek the inner beauty that Chrysostom writes we ought to seek. Again, we want them to seek this inner beauty because it is a matter of life and death and it stands at the very fabric of who and what they are and will become and whether they will be able to say yes to Christ in this life, so that when He offers them eternal life at the Judgment Seat they will again be able to say yes to Christ.

When working with young people, one often hears the words, "it depends"—"it depends on the circumstances," "it may be wrong for me, but not others," "I would not do it, but I can not judge what others think," "as long as nobody gets hurt," etc. On the other hand, the Holy Scripture confronts us with statements and even lists of what is and is not acceptable behavior. One who studies and believes the Word of God is compelled to deal with the fact that there is objective truth and objective right and wrong in the Scripture. Understanding that God lays before us a way of life in the Scripture and seeks that we choose the path

---

[42] St. John Chrysostom, "After Eutropius having been found outside the Church had been taken Captive," Homily 2:17, Translated by Rev. W.R.W. Stephens *Nicene and Post-Nicene Fathers*—Volume 9., reproduced in *FaithWorx* [CD-Rom] (Theologic Systems Electronic Reference Library, http://www.theologic.com, Version 2.0, 1998).

which leads to life, the following pages will explore what the scripture lays before us as expectations for how we ought to live our life.

Moral and Ethical Lists

The New Testament clearly requires that one lives out or puts into practice the teachings of Jesus Christ. In Matthew 5:19 Jesus places the emphasis on doing His commandments as He also does in Mark 3:35 and in Luke 6:46. Jesus was the first Christian Ethicist. To believe what Christ said was only the beginning; He expected that what He taught would bring about a change in how people lived out their lives.[43] Both the New and Old Testament contain lists of ethical behavior, dealing with behavior and disposition towards others. "There are lists of commandments and offenses, numerical lists of moral wisdom, lists of virtues and vices, and lists of duties in the household (Haustafeln) or the community (Gemeindetafeln)."[44] Ethical lists from both the Old and New Testament set the stage and standard for behavioral expectations for young and old alike. Some of these lists, such as the Ten Commandments and the Sermon on the Mount, are well known, while others are perhaps unfamiliar to the general reader, though they have had an effect on the Church's teaching of right and wrong behavior.

The most well know list of expected behavior is *The Ten Commandments* (Exodus 20:2-17). Another Old Testament example of ethical lists is the twelve crimes that bring the curse of God found in Deuteronomy 27:15 - 28:2 dealing with relationships with ones family and neighbors. Other examples of ethical lists in the Old Testament can be found in *sexual offenses* listed in Leviticus18:20-30, much of which affects to this day our measure of appropriate sexual relations. This list deals with sexual relations, adultery, homosexuality, bestiality and paganism. There are other ethical lists in the Old Testament, such as those found in Exodus 21:12, 15-17; 22:18, 19; 31:15, Nehemiah 10:28-39, Ezekiel 18:5-18; Job 31:1-40; 1, Samuel 12:2-5; Psalms 15:2-5; 24:3-6; Isaiah 33:14-16; Micah 6:6-8, Proverbs 6.16-19; 30.11-14; and Amos 1.3-3.2.

The New Testament likewise contains several ethical lists of virtues and duties in the household and in the community. Lists of virtue can be found in many of St. Paul's letters. Many of these lists were addressing specific issues taking place within the particular communities to which Paul was writing such as found in Gal 5:19-23; I Cor 5:10-11; 6:9-10; 2 Cor 12:20; Rom 13:13. Paul writes that love must permeate the Christians ethical conduct and exhorts Christians to live a virtuous life guided by the Holy Spirit (Rom 8:15-15). For Paul, the community was essential to living the Christian life. Members of the community were there to help one another in good times and bad. They were also there to hold each other accountable. Paul writes to the Galatians,

> For the whole law is fulfilled in one word, "You shall love your neighbor as yourself."
> But if you bite and devour one another take heed that you are not consumed by one another.
> But I say, walk by the Spirit, and do not gratify the desires of the flesh. For the desires of the flesh are against the Spirit, and the desires of the Spirit are against the flesh; for these are opposed to each other, to prevent you from doing what you would. But if you are led by the

---

[43] Stanley Samuel Harakas, *Living The Faith: The Praxis of Eastern Orthodox Ethics*, Minneapolis, Minnesota (Light and Life Publishing Company, 1992), 3.

[44] Verhi, "Ethical Lists," The Oxford Companion to the Bible, 201.

Spirit you are not under the law. Now the works of the flesh are plain: fornication, impurity, licentiousness, idolatry, sorcery, enmity, strife, jealousy, anger, selfishness, dissension, party spirit, envy, drunkenness, carousing, and the like. I warn you, as I warned you before, that those who do such things shall not inherit the kingdom of God. But the fruit of the Spirit is love, joy, peace, patience, kindness, goodness, faithfulness, gentleness, self-control; against such there is no law. And those who belong to Christ Jesus have crucified the flesh with its passions and desires.

If we live by the Spirit, let us also walk by the Spirit. Let us have no self-conceit, no provoking of one another, no envy of one another.Brethren, if a man is overtaken in any trespass, you who are spiritual should restore him in a spirit of gentleness. Look to yourself, lest you too be tempted. Bear one another's burdens, and so fulfill the law of Christ. (*Galatians 5:14 - 6:2*)[45]

To Timothy he adds,

So shun youthful passions and aim at righteousness, faith, love, and peace, along with those who call upon the Lord from a pure heart. Have nothing to do with stupid, senseless controversies; you know that they breed quarrels. And the Lord's servant must not be quarrelsome but kindly to every one, an apt teacher, forbearing, correcting his opponents with gentleness. God may perhaps grant that they will repent and come to know the truth, and they may escape from the snare of the devil, after being captured by him to do his will.

But understand this, that in the last days there will come times of stress. For men will be lovers of self, lovers of money, proud, arrogant, abusive, disobedient to their parents, ungrateful, unholy, inhuman, implacable, slanderers, profligates, fierce, haters of good, treacherous, reckless, swollen with conceit, lovers of pleasure rather than lovers of God, holding the form of religion but denying the power of it. Avoid such people. (*2 Timothy 2:22 - 3:5*)

Other New Testament writers also used ethical lists in their writings. St. Peter writes, "So put away all malice and all guile and insincerity and envy and all slander." (*1 Peter 2:1*). Again he writes, "Let the time that is past suffice for doing what the Gentiles like to do, living in licentiousness, passions, drunkenness, revels, carousing, and lawless idolatry." (*1 Peter 4:3*) "But let none of you suffer as a murderer, or a thief, or a wrongdoer, or a mischief-maker;" (*1 Peter 4:15*) We read in the Book of Revelation, "But as for the cowardly, the faithless, the polluted, as for murderers, fornicators, sorcerers, idolaters, and all liars, their lot shall be in the lake that burns with fire and sulphur, which is the second death." (*Revelation 21:8*) "Outside are the dogs and sorcerers and fornicators and murderers and idolaters, and every one who loves and practices falsehood." (*Revelation 22:15*)

Aside from ethical lists of virtues, the New Testament presents us with lists of duties in the household and community. Perhaps the best known of these is the text that is used in the Orthodox Christian Marriage Service, where Paul outlines the expected relationship between a husband and wife in Ephesians 5:20-33.

Paul continues, in Ephesians 6:1-4, his lists of duties in the household by adding in expectations of how children ought to behave to their parents and how parents ought to treat their children. The Church also expects that the elders set the example of that right behavior so that the younger members of the community can learn by their example. In Timothy Paul

---

[45] See also: Ephesians 4:25 - 5:7 and Colossians 3:12 - 17

outlines what is expected of bishops, as they stand as an example in the community, as to how others ought to live.

> The saying is sure: If any one aspires to the office of bishop, he desires a noble task. Now a bishop must be above reproach, the husband of one wife, temperate, sensible, dignified, and hospitable, an apt teacher, no drunkard, not violent but gentle, not quarrelsome, and no lover of money. He must manage his own household well, keeping his children submissive and respectful in every way; for if a man does not know how to manage his own household, how can he care for God's church? He must not be a recent convert, or he may be puffed up with conceit and fall into the condemnation of the devil; moreover he must be well thought of by outsiders, or he may fall into reproach and the snare of the devil. (*1 Timothy 3:1-13*)

St. Paul goes on in his letter to Titus to outline how people within the community ought to respect and treat one another. Moreover St. Paul tells the older members to act accordingly so that they might be a good example to the younger members of the Community. Here, St. Paul is of the mind that the younger members of the community learn how they ought to act by the example set by the older members.

> Bid the older men be temperate, serious, sensible, sound in faith, in love, and in steadfastness. Bid the older women likewise to be reverent in behavior, not to be slanderers or slaves to drink; they are to teach what is good, and so train the young women to love their husbands and children, to be sensible, chaste, domestic, kind, and submissive to their husbands, that the word of God may not be discredited. Likewise urge the younger men to control themselves. Show yourself in all respects a model of good deeds, and in your teaching show integrity, gravity, and sound speech that cannot be censured, so that an opponent may be put to shame, having nothing evil to say of us. (*Titus 2:2 - 8*)

Peter, like Paul, reminds the elders how they ought to act in 1 Peter 5:1-4 and he adds that the younger members likewise need to show respect to their elders.

> Likewise you that are younger be subject to the elders. Clothe yourselves, all of you, with humility toward one another, for "God opposes the proud, but gives grace to the humble." Humble yourselves therefore under the mighty hand of God, that in due time he may exalt you. (*1 Peter 5:5 - 6*)

It is clear from the scriptures that the Christian community has expectations of what is right behavior. Educating the young has been a focus of the community of the people of God from the earliest time. Proverbs tells us that the mother was a teacher to her children. "My son, keep your father's commandment, and forsake not your mother's teaching." (*Proverbs 6:20*) The practice appears to continue with the early church as recorded in the second letter of Timothy. "I am reminded of your sincere faith, a faith that dwelt first in your grandmother Lois and your mother Eunice and now, I am sure, dwells in you." (*2 Timothy 1:5*)

From Old and New Testament times, the practice of religious education began early in the life of a child. The home played an integral part in the educational process, as did the entire community by example and encouragement. While we try to accomplish the same today by our Christian Education Programs, Youth Ministry, and participation in the Divine

Liturgical Services, both the Church and family need to work more closely together in the nurturing of children and young people who belong to the Christian Community.

Throughout this chapter, it has been shown that there are specific teachings in the scripture of what is right and what is wrong. Many of the issues raised in *The Orthodox Teen Survey* have clear references and teachings in the Scripture. It would seem that members of the Christian Community are at least compelled to read the inspired Word of God in the Scriptures and formulate their position on current moral and ethical issues on that Word. Whether the current issues are getting along with parents, pre-marital sex, homosexuality, violence, adultery, abortion, alcohol abuse, drug abuse, and so forth, all of which the Scriptures address, a member of Christ's Body, it would seem, cannot simply ignore the scriptural teachings on these issues. The New Testament Scripture, as the inspired Word of God, was written within the Christian Community for members of the Christian Community, in order to help deepen their faith and understanding of the Resurrected Lord and to help them live life. It is in understanding and coming into relationship with the Resurrected Lord that one understands that life cannot help but be changed by this relationship. This changed and new life compels members of the Christian Community to care about what other members of the Christian Community think, what they believe, and what they do. Christians are called to care and to help one another in the life long process of working on salvation. If Christians love one another then they will care for one another's salvation. Patriarch Bartholomew I, writes, "According to Dostoevsky's Starets Zosima in the Brothers Karamazov, each of us is responsible for everyone and everything." AndWhen we become sensitive to God's world around us, we grow more conscious also of God's world within us."[46]

Mission Statement for Youth Ministry—Antiochian Orthodox Christian Archdiocese

The proceeding pages have concerned themselves with the biblical perspective of why youth need be nurtured by the Christian Community, what is expected of young people and expected of those who both minister to them and are present in their lives. As a means of synthesizing the Biblical and Theological perspective of youth ministry, the Antiochian Orthodox Christian Archdiocese has set forth the following principles for its youth and youth workers to help maintain their focus in ministry. This Mission statement stands here as a measurement of where youth are and where the Church desires to move young people when looking at the information derived from *The Orthodox Teen Survey*. It is the writers belief that this mission statement capturers the Biblical perspective written of earlier in this chapter. It is the writer's intention not simply to move our youth to produce better statistics than those found in other surveys, but to move them into a stronger and healthier relationship with one another, with their parents, in their communities, in the Church and ultimately with God. This mission statement lays the foundation for that journey.

---

[46]Patriach Barthomlemeu, "Stewards of Creation," *The Orthodox Church,* September/October 1997, 3.

Living the Orthodox Faith In Christ Through Worship, Witness, Service and Fellowship[47]

In July of 1990, Metropolitan PHILIP[48], out of a concern for the well being of the youth of the Antiochian Orthodox Christian Archdiocese of North America, asked the newly appointed archdiocese co-youth directors, Frs. Joseph Purpura and George Geha, to convene a three day working conference at the Antiochian Village in Ligonier, Pennsylvania, to redefine the purpose and goals of youth ministry in the Archdiocese. This gathering consisted of the Archdiocese Youth Directors, the Regional and North American Spiritual Advisors and Presidents of Teen and Senior SOYO,[49] as well as the director of Campus Ministry, the director of the department of Christian Education, and others in the Archdiocese involved in the youth movement. At this meeting a Mission Statement of Youth Ministry was produced along with an administrative action plan. During the design of this mission statement, it was important to the drafters of this statement that it be well understood that what was intended was to enable our young people to live their Orthodox Faith every moment of their lives. One's faith should permeate every aspect of life, whether it is at home, school, work, or the Church. Of significance here are the words "in Christ." It was essential to the drafters that it be understood that Christ is the measure of right and wrong or whether we are, living the faith or not living the faith. It was essential to the drafters of this mission statement that it be understood that the emphasis in this ministry be based upon Jesus Christ, who He is and what that means for one's own life. Scripture references such as Matthew 28:20, Mark 8:29, John 4:25-26, 4:25-26, 6:44-51, 8:12, 8:58, 10:7-18, 10:31-39, 11:25-26, 14:6-7, 15:1-10 and 20:11-18, which refer to who Christ is and what that implies were much in the minds of the drafters.

Statement of Purpose

> We believe that the Goal of Orthodox Christian Youth Ministry is the integration of each young person fully into the total life of the Church. We believe that Orthodox Christians must commit themselves to living the Orthodox Faith daily. Worship, Witness, Service and Fellowship are the natural expressions of that commitment. We define them as follows:[50]

Keeping in mind that one cannot run a race successfully unless one knows where the finish line is, the goal here is to enable the young person to become fully involved in the life of the Church in all of Her aspects and with all the implications of being a member of the body of Christ. Participation in the life of the Church expresses itself in a variety of ways. Living the faith on a daily basis has been categorized into four areas that the authors felt summed up that life, but in no way is meant to be all inclusive and exclusionary of other terms that may be implied or used in the Church.

---

[47] "Youth Ministry Platform of the Antiochian Orthodox Christian Archdiocese of North America"

[48] Metropolitan PHILIP (Saliba) is the Primate of the Antiochian Orthodox Christian Archdiocese of North America (1966 to present).

[49] Senior SOYO, now called the Fellowship of St. John the Divine, was for people ages 19 and above. Teen SOYO then and now is for teenagers 13-19 years of age.

[50] Youth Ministry Platform.

WORSHIP - For Orthodox Christians, corporate worship is the sacramental expression of and participation in Holy Tradition, and is the indispensable foundation of youth ministry at all levels. Upon this foundation, we must cultivate a daily personal prayer life and reading of Holy Scripture.[51]

Worship stands as the essential beginning, foundation, and ongoing expression of life in Christ. It is the source of life, strength, and nourishment, a reference point for one's relationship with God. It is explicitly understood that worship of the one true Living God is essential to a relationship with Him. A person's prayer life, reading of the scripture as God's Word, and participation in the corporate worship of the Church community, culminating in the reception of the Eucharist as the very Body and Blood of our Lord and Savior Jesus Christ all stand as defining actions of membership in the Church as the very Body of Christ. We want our young people to be fully immersed in the worshipping life of the community. It is in worship of God that we become one with one another and one with God. We want our young people to understand the beauty and depth of worship and the deep impact that it can have on them as a human person created in the image and likeness of God. Worship is essential not simply as an obligation but as a defining point of whom and what we are (Matthew 4:10, John 4:20-26, Romans 12:1, Exodus 15:2, Psalms 7:17, 30:12, 104:33 and 34:1). Worship enables us to do good and we want to strengthen our young people to avoid evil and to do good instead (Psalms 119:7, 119:108,119:171 and Romans 12:9-12). Worship allows us to give thanks to God, to be grateful for all that He does for us and to continuously be mindful of Him and His teachings. We want our young people to always be mindful of God, who He is and who they are in relation to Him. Being conscious of God's presence at all times enables us to discern and make good choices.

WITNESS - Christ calls us to be His witness in the world. We must enable our youth to express their faith for themselves and to others in order to be true witnesses to Christ and the Orthodox Faith.[52]

Christ commands all of us to bear witness to him and glorify His Father. Jesus says, "For whoever is ashamed of me and of my words in this adulterous and sinful generation, of him will the Son of man also be ashamed, when he comes in the glory of his Father with the holy angels." *(Mark 8:38).* We want our young people to find strength and courage in the teachings of our Lord rather than feeling embarrassed or feeling strange about sharing what they believe. We want to show that it makes a difference in how they express their lives. We want our young people to feel good and strong about saying, "I want to do good because I love God", "I choose not to do that because it will not please God," "I genuinely care about you because you are my brother or sister in Christ." For teens bearing Witness to Christ is perhaps one of the most difficult actions for a young person to do through their teen years. Being different as St. Peter calls us to be, for some teens is tantamount to estranging

---

[51] Ibid.
[52] Ibid.

themselves from their peer groups and not being part of the "in-crowd." We want our teens to find strength in being different from this fallen world, and to know that being different in fact is being human, as God has created us to be. We want to create support groups and systems where teens can feel supported in doing that which is right. Bearing Witness to Christ amongst their peers is essential not only for their own salvation and healthy life, but for those around them who need peers that set the right example of healthy living and relationships. There are many scriptural passages that remind us of our need to bear witness, at all times in our life:

> A new commandment I give to you, that you love one another; even as I have loved you, that you also love one another. By this all men will know that you are my disciples, if you have love for one another." (*John 13:34*)
> Command and teach these things. Let no one despise your youth, but set the believers an example in speech and conduct, in love, in faith, in purity. Till I come, attend to the public reading of scripture, to preaching, to teaching. Do not neglect the gift you have, which was given you by prophetic utterance when the council of elders laid their hands upon you. Practice these duties, devote yourself to them, so that all may see your progress. Take heed to yourself and to your teaching; hold to that, for by so doing you will save both yourself and your hearers. *(1 Timothy 4:11-16)*Show yourself in all respects a model of good deeds, and in your teaching show integrity, gravity, [8]and sound speech that cannot be censured, so that an opponent may be put to shame, having nothing evil to say of us. *(Titus 2:7-8)*

SERVICE - Christ came not to be served, but to serve. We need to move our youth to do the same. We honor and glorify God by loving and serving mankind in the name of Jesus Christ, using our God-given gifts and talents.[53]

Our Lord sets the example of how he expects us to serve. We are called to serve all and to bear witness to Christ in that service. We want our young people to recognize that everything they have is a gift from God and with that gift comes the expectation that they will utilize it for the benefit of those around them. It is in the sharing of these gifts that one finds their value and meaning. In freely sharing our gifts of talents and resources, our young people give thanks to God by emulating His free giving. It is in this act of thanksgiving and serving that young people value those around them and hence find their own identity. We find ourselves, not within us, but in how we interact with others, hence we find ourselves in others. This is much like the saying, "One can not be a Christian alone"—because it is in the other that we are able to express our love for God. Matthew writes:

> But Jesus called them to him and said, "You know that the rulers of the Gentiles lord it over them, and their great men exercise authority over them. It shall not be so among you; but whoever would be great among you must be your servant, and whoever would be first among you must be your slave; even as the Son of man came not to be served but to serve, and to give his life as a ransom for many." *(Matthew 20:25-28)*

Matthew later offers the quintessential statement on service in chapter 25, where he describes all its expressions as service done as if to Christ Himself.[54]

---

[53] Ibid.
[54] Matthew 25:31-46

God calls all of us to serve, even those who blaspheme his Name and persecute his followers, like Saul (St. Paul). Some think it is only the perfect that should approach the service of God, but God often calls us out of the depth of our weakness and sinfulness to serve, be healed, and be one with Him. We want our young people to understand the great depth of God's Love for us. God always desires that we be one with Him and He welcomes us. We want our young people to understand that despite whatever one may have done, God still desires that we repent and come to Him.

> **FELLOWSHIP** - The Holy Trinity is the perfect model of fellowship; the Father, Son, and Holy Spirit share perfect communion and exists in perfect love as a community. By gathering together in fellowship, and by showing love for one another in Christ, we emulate the life of the Holy Trinity in our daily life.[55]

Fellowship finds itself as the fourth item, not because it is least in importance, but because it is understood as a natural outcome of the first three actions mentioned above. We find and enjoy fellowship with one another because we share in common worship, we bear witness to the same God and we work together. Hence we know one another, we think alike, we have the same goals, and we have the same Father, the same Spirit, and are adopted as children of God because of the same Son. We find meaning in fellowship because we are one in Christ. The Disciples gathered in the early Church to worship, listen to the apostle's teachings and to share fellowship with one another. We likewise want the same for our young people. Fellowship in the Church is radically different than that of the world, because it is based on our relationship with Christ. We want our young people to perceive and understand that the fellowship they enjoy with one another in the Church community is different because it is based on a relationship with Christ in Love and Truth and that that relationship compels us to act differently.

> That which was from the beginning, which we have heard, which we have seen with our eyes, which we have looked upon and touched with our hands, concerning the word of life—the life was made manifest, and we saw it, and testify to it, and proclaim to you the eternal life which was with the Father and was made manifest to us—that which we have seen and heard we proclaim also to you, so that you may have fellowship with us; and our fellowship is with the Father and with his Son Jesus Christ. And we are writing this that our joy may be complete. *(1 John 1:1-4)*

Keeping in mind that our goal is to change lives and bring about committed relationship with Christ and His Church,

> **Our ultimate goal** must be to see that our youth grow to love Christ and His Church and to pursue a righteous way of life.[56]

---

[55] Youth Ministry Platform.
[56] Ibid.

We call our young people to, "live their Orthodox Faith on a daily basis in Christ," so that they will be changed, be one with God and live their lives accordingly. All that we do and say with them should move them into a closer and stronger relationship with Jesus Christ. Youth Ministry should ultimately bring about change for the good in the youth on whom it is focused. Unless change is brought about in young people's lives, unless a new way of thinking that means a radical divergence from the ways of this world to one in which young people see the world through the eyes of Christ, which enables them to discern the lies perpetrated on the world by Satan and those who choose the way of death, then we have missed the mark in enabling young people to live life. The fact that our young people are Christians should have a profound impact on how and why they make their decisions in daily life. This desire to choose *rightly* should be motivated out of a love for Christ, His Church and a desire to be one with Him.

> **Our movement** integrates the Camping Programs, Teen SOYO, Campus Ministry and the Fellowship of St. John the Divine - programs designed to meet the needs of varying age groups. We will attain these goals by training youth ministers, both clergy and lay, to serve at all levels, and by developing and providing relevant resource materials.[57]

In conclusion, the Youth Ministry Mission Statement of the Antiochian Orthodox Christian Archdiocese recognizes that change does not simply happen on its own. It happens because persons come to know those to whom they are ministering, their needs, wants, likes, dislikes, fears, concerns and chooses to enter into their lives for their benefit. It likewise recognizes that those who are called to minister to young people themselves have a love for Christ, His Church and the teens they are called to serve; and prepare themselves on an ongoing basis for that ministry. Recognizing this need, in the next chapter we turn our attention to the young people, where they are, what they believe, what they fear, what they think, as well as their perception of the adults and Church in their lives. In the words of Metropolitan PHILIP[58], we will, "plunge into the depths."

---

[57] Ibid.

[58] Metropolitan PHILIP (Saliba) quote is from his sermons given on various occasions.

CHAPTER 3
SURVEY OF ORTHODOX CHRISTIAN TEENS ACROSS NORTH AMERICA

In an effort to better understand and minister to Teens, a 214-question survey was designed and administered to Orthodox Christian teens across the United States and Canada. This survey was designed to identify major issues confronting teens in their daily life. The hope is that the survey results will serve as a tool for those ministering to teens by identifying areas that need attention from the Church and from those ministering to and with teens.

The process of developing this survey was multi-leveled. Past surveys were studied and pertinent questions were either used in whole, part, or re-written for current trends and issues. This was done to build a base of questions, which could be used as comparison with other studies. This first step led to a base of less than 30 percent of the questions. The second step was to add the questions that came out of the author's personal experience of working with teens over the past twenty years. Third, meetings were held with the seven regional Teen SOYO[59] Spiritual Advisors of the Antiochian Orthodox Christian Archdiocese of North America, the seven regional Archdiocese Youth Directors, the North American Spiritual Advisor of Teen SOYO, as well as Teens themselves, to review, critique, add to the list of questions, and even drop some of the questions from the list. Over the course of several months, this process led to the development of *The Orthodox Teen Survey* consisting of 214 questions.

The Survey was administered over the course of six months (March—August 1998). The surveys were administered to teens in attendance at Delegates Meetings, Conferences and Camping programs of the Antiochian Orthodox Christian Archdiocese. This meant that the typical teen in the survey was active in some form or another in the life of the Church. In many ways this survey is about the teens that we are reaching through the various vehicles of the Church. The environment in which the surveys were administered provided a quiet atmosphere and privacy for each teen. No names or other identifying marks appeared on the surveys that would allow for the identification of any individual teen. Once completed, the teens themselves placed their surveys in a box, which was sealed once the last survey was placed in it. The completed surveys were then sent directly to the Department of Youth Ministry of the Antiochian Orthodox Christian Archdiocese, where the data from each survey was entered into a database to manage this information. The database used was a custom database written in Microsoft Access specifically for this survey. Survey

---

[59] SOYO is the official youth organization of the Antiochian Orthodox Christian Archdiocese of North America. SOYO stands for "Society of Orthodox Youth". Some convert parishes that have come into the Archdiocese in the past ten years have entered with existing youth groups and do not yet use the name "SOYO" but fully participate in the Youth Movement of the Archdiocese and they are included in the 83%.

reports, which appear in this project, are a result of the compilation of the data collected through *The Orthodox Teen Survey*.

This chapter will focus on the data itself. The purpose of presenting this data is to present a picture of where these particular teens were at the time of the survey in their thinking, beliefs, and behavior. It is not the purpose of this survey to assess whether the teens are "good" or "poor" Christians. It is hoped that this data will be used as a tool to help teens move further along in their journey of developing a deeper and more meaningful relationship with Jesus Christ, His Church and those around them. The next chapter will deal with the Church's teaching on some of the major issues raised in this chapter. Due to limitations of space and time the results of the data will be highlighted and significant correlations and parallels with other areas of the data will be made. The reader is encouraged to take time to study the complete report contained in the appendix of this project.

Survey Results

Participants

Surveys from 790 teens were entered into the database. Of those 790 surveys the following demographic information was compiled as detailed in the charts below:

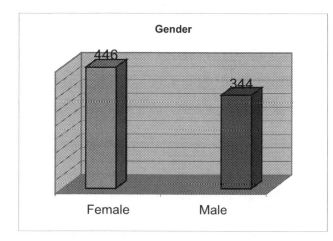

446 Females and 344 Males participated in the survey.

The majority of teens were between the ages of 13—17.

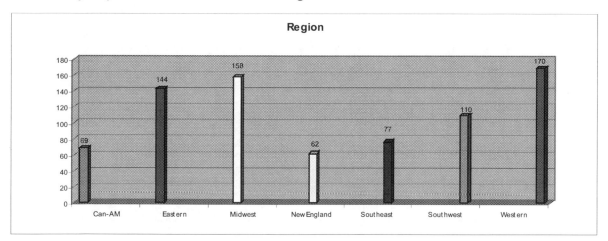

The number of participants from each region of the Antiochian Archdiocese (United States and Canada) was consistent with the size of each region.

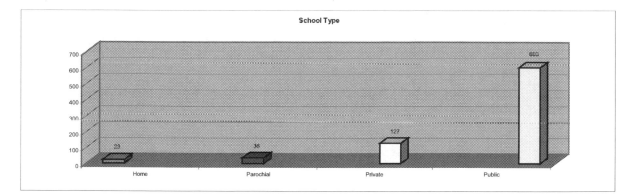

31

Joseph F. Purpura

Seventy-six percent (76%) of the teens in the survey attended public schools, while another 16 percent attended private schools, 4.6 percent attended Parochial Schools, while 2.9 percent were home schooled.

•It should be noted that 83 percent of the teens in this survey are members of their Parish Teen SOYO Movement (Youth Group).

Parent's Religion

Nearly 93 percent of teens reported that their mother was an Orthodox Christian and 88 percent reported that their father was an Orthodox Christian.

Mother's Religion	Number	Percentage
Orthodox Christian	733	92.78%
Roman Catholic	33	4.18%
No Faith	10	1.27%
Lutheran	3	0.38%
Presbyterian	2	0.25%
Maronite	2	0.25%
Episcopal	2	0.25%
Protestant	1	0.13%
Muslim	1	0.13%
Eastern Catholic	1	0.13%
Baptist	1	0.13%
Agnostic	1	0.13%

Father's Religion	Number	Percentage
Orthodox Christian	696	88.10%
Roman Catholic	37	4.68%
No Faith	27	3.42%
Do not know my father's religion	7	0.89%
Protestant	4	0.51%
Atheist	3	0.38%
Methodist	3	0.38%
Lutheran	2	0.25%
Baptist	2	0.25%
Jewish	2	0.25%
Agnostic	1	0.13%
Episcopal	1	0.13%
Calvinist	1	0.13%
Muslim	1	0.13%
Pentecostal	1	0.13%
Armenian	1	0.13%
Jehovah Witness	1	0.13%

Family Observance of the Major Fasts and Prayers at Meals

Of the teens in the survey, 83 percent reported that they attended Church at least once weekly. Just over 54 percent of families in the survey observed the Fast prior to Christmas (November 15th—December 24th), while over 82 percent observed the fast of Great Lent (40 days prior to Holy Week and Holy Week itself leading up to Pascha [Easter]). Before eating dinner, 57 percent of families say a prayer. Of the teens in the survey 48 percent report praying alone *frequently*, while another 39 percent report praying alone *occasionally*. Given the significance of prayer life in the Christian community, this is an area to which we want to give attention. Also, to further develop the prayer and fasting lives of our teens and families, particularly since the Church stresses the importance of prayer life and even modern studies speak to the significance and power of prayer.[60]

---

[60] Usha Lee McFarling, "Power of faith might be good for what ails you, science says," *The Boston Globe*, 27 December 1998, A12.

Joseph F. Purpura

Parental Discussion

Time spent in parent/teen discussion was an area of the survey that appeared to show significant impact on the outcome of teen relations and behavior. When asked about their parent's involvement in their life teens reported:

Issue	Percent who said Yes
My family is helpful to me with my homework	85%[61]
My family openly talks about issues that concern me	79%

My Parents have discussed with me their feelings about—	
Pre-Marital Sexual relations	69%
Birth Control	38%
Abortion	59%
Euthanasia	35%
Homosexuality	63%
Aids and other sexually transmitted diseases	65%
Stealing	85%
Lying	94%
Truthfulness	96%
School grades	98%
Their expectations for my career	76%
Their expectations for my life	76%
Marriage	71%
Fidelity (or faithfulness) in Marriage	64%
Dating	81%
Their Religious Faith	86%

My Family discusses with me issues concerning	
Our community	69%
Our Church	88%
The World	81%
Me	94%
Other family members	91%
My school day	82%
Family problems and interests	89%
News and current events	80%
School in general	96%

[61] Where only whole numbers are shown, numbers are rounded up or down using the standard formula of less than .5 rounds down and .5 or greater rounds up to the nearest whole number.

Parent Teen Relations

How well would you say you get along with your parents …	
Very well	46%
Fairly well	47%
Not well at all	6%

Would you say you get along better with your mother or father?	
Mother	34%
Father	21%
Both	41%
Neither	4%

My parent's involvement in my life is …	
Not enough	7%
Just right	73%
Too much	19%

The majority of teens in the survey came from homes where their birth parents were married to each other.

My birth parents are…	
Married to each other	87.09%
Divorced	8.73%
Father deceased	1.77%
Separated	.89%
Never married	.63%
Mother deceased	.13%

A majority of teens arrive home from school with an adult present to greet them or supervise their activities.

When you arrive home from school is there an adult there?	
Yes	61%
No	33%
Sometimes	3%

How teens spend their time

On average how much time do you spend each day on a computer?	
None	17%
Less than 1 hour	34%
1-2 hours	36%
3-4 hours	9%
More than 4 hours	3%

On average how much time do you spend each day on the Internet?	
None	38%
Less than 1 hour	34%
1-2 hours	22%
3-4 hours	4%
More than 4 hours	3%

On average how much time do you spend each day in an on-line chat room?	
None	65%
Less than 1 hour	25%
1-2 hours	8%
3-4 hours	2%
More than 4 hours	1%

The vast majority of teens are somewhat satisfied with their lives

In general, are you satisfied or dissatisfied with the way things are going in your personal life?	
Very Satisfied	34%
Somewhat Satisfied	58%
Dissatisfied	8%

Teen Behaviors in the Past Month

Tobacco	
I smoked cigarettes	
None	79%
1-2 Times	7%
2-6 Times	7%
More than 6 Times	6%
I smoked cigars	
None	88%
1-2 Times	7%
2-6 Times	4%
More than 6 Times	1%
I chewed tobacco	
None	97%
1-2 Times	1%
2-6 Times	1%
More than 6 Times	1%

Teen Behaviors in the Past Twelve Months

Alcohol	
I have drunk alcohol with my friends	
None	57%
1-2 Times	13%
2-6 Times	17%
More than 6 Times	12%
I have drunk alcohol by myself	
None	83%
1-2 Times	8%
2-6 Times	5%
More than 6 Times	3%

Teen Behaviors in their Lifetime

Drugs	
I have smoked marijuana	
Never	82%
1-2 Times	7%
2-6 Times	4%
More than 6 Times	6%
I have used cocaine	
Never	97.0%
1-2 Times	.38%
2-6 Times	.89%
More than 6 Times	.63%
I have tried other illegal drugs (other than marijuana and cocaine)	
Never	94.30%
1-2 Times	2.28%
2-6 Times	1.39%
More than 6 Times	1.52%
I have smoked cigarettes	
Never	52%
1-2 Times	14%
2-6 Times	14%
More than 6 Times	20%
I have chewed tobacco	
Never	92%
1-2 Times	4%
2-6 Times	2%
More than 6 Times	2%

Teens believe that it is the individual people they associate with that affects how they think and behave.

What do teens believe influences them.

I am very influenced by... (Teens were asked to rate how much each of these sources influenced them, the following is the percent who rated each source as influencing them "very much")	
Religion	72%
My Parents	67%
Friends	59%
School	48%
Church Youth Group	46%
Pastor	44%
Church Youth Worker	30%
School Teachers	26%
Music	22%
Church School Teachers	22%
Guidance Counselor	16%
Television	13%
Movies	12%
Books	12%
Computers	12%
Magazines	8%
The Internet	7%

Greatest Problems Facing Teens

When teens were asked to identify the three greatest problems they faced, their friends faced and their peers in general faced, in order of significance, they reported them in the following order:

Greatest Problems facing me, my best friends, and my peers		
Me	**My best friend**	**My peers**
School Grades	School Grades	Being Liked
Being Liked	Being Liked	Peer Pressures
Fears	Getting Along with Parents	Drug Abuse
Getting Along with Parents	Peer Pressures	Pressure to Have Sex
Career Uncertainties	School Problems	School Grades
Peer Pressures	Pressure to Have Sex	Getting Along with Parents
Weight Problems	Weight Problems	Alcohol Abuse
School Problems	Growing Pains	Teen Pregnancy
Financing College	Depression	School Problems
Depression	Financing College	Depression
Pressure to Have Sex	Drug Abuse	Weight Problems
Growing Pains	Teen Pregnancy	Career Uncertainties

What Teens Believe are Right and Wrong Behaviors

Is it right or wrong to have an abortion for reasons other than to save the physical life of the mother?

What Teens Believe are Right and Wrong Behaviors	
Right	5%
Wrong	67%
Not Sure	27%

Is it right or wrong to have an abortion to save the physical life of the mother?[62]

Right	38%
Wrong	20%
Not Sure	41%

Is it right or wrong to have an abortion for any reason?

Right	3%
Wrong	63%
Not Sure	33%

Is it right or wrong for two sixteen year olds who love each other to have sexual intercourse before they are married?

Right	8%
Wrong	68%
Not Sure	23%

Is it right or wrong to have sexual intercourse before you are married?

Right	6%
Wrong	68%
Not Sure	26%

Is it right or wrong to use birth control before you are married?

Right	18%
Wrong	40%
Not Sure	41%

Is it right or wrong to have homosexual relationships?

Right	6%
Wrong	69%
Not Sure	23%

Is it right or wrong for you to have sex with someone of the same sex as you?

Right	1%
Wrong	87%
Not Sure	11%

Is it right or wrong for someone else to have sex with someone of the same sex as him or her?

Right	3%
Wrong	78%

---

[62] The question was phrased this way due to the consensus in the Orthodox Church that it may be understandable for a couple, in consultation with their Spiritual Father, to choose to have an abortion when this is the only way to save the physical life of the mother. The rationale is that in effect the attempt is being made to at least save one of the two lives that are threatened. Here the emphasis is on saving a life not choosing to end one.

What Teens Believe are Right and Wrong Behaviors

Not Sure	17%

Is it right or wrong to look at pornographic material?

Right	5%
Wrong	64%
Not Sure	29%

Is it right or wrong to have "cyber sex" with someone in a computer chat room on the Internet?

Right	4%
Wrong	72%
Not Sure	23%

Is it right or wrong when you are married to have a sexual relationship with someone other than the person you are married?

Right	2%
Wrong	92%
Not Sure	5%

Is it right or wrong to lie to one's parent?

Right	2%
Wrong	81%
Not Sure	16%

Is it right or wrong to cheat on a test at school?

Right	3%
Wrong	78%
Not Sure	19%

Is it right or wrong for sixteen-year-olds to drink a couple of beers at a party?

Right	7%
Wrong	61%
Not Sure	32%

Is it right or wrong to steal clothes from a store that I know makes a lot of money?

Right	0.63%
Wrong	93%
Not Sure	5%

Is Capital Punishment (putting someone to death for a crime they have committed) right or wrong?

Right	21%
Wrong	37%
Not Sure	41%

Is Euthanasia (Helping someone who is ill end their life to free them from suffering or because they are elderly and feel they have no more to offer) right or wrong?

Right	18%
Wrong	46%
Not Sure	35%

What Teens Believe are Right and Wrong Behaviors

Is it right or wrong to help those who are less fortunate than you?

Right	93%
Wrong	2%
Not Sure	3%

Is it right or wrong to help someone stand up against injustice, when you will not gain anything from doing so?

Right	79%
Wrong	5%
Not Sure	15%

Dating and Related Issues

How many times in the past twelve months have you been out on a date (such as going to a party or movie with one person of the opposite sex)?

None	33%
1-2 Times	19%
3-5 Times	15%
6-9 Times	9%
10-19 Times	10%
20 Times or More	13%

Is it difficult for you to talk to other teens of the opposite sex?

Yes	13%
Sometimes	2%
No	85%

How often do you think about sex?

Very Often	21%
Sometimes	62%
Never	17%

Have you ever had sexual intercourse ("gone all the way" or "made love")?

Never	95.44%
Yes, 1 Time	0.76%
Yes, 2-5 Times	1.52%
Yes, 6 Times or more	1.01%
I do not know what sexual intercourse is	0.51%

Have you ever been forced to have a sexual relationship you did not want?

Yes	6%
No	94%

Have you ever been sexually harassed?

Yes	22%
No	78%

Dating and Related Issues	
Teen Pregnancy—If you are a female, have you ever been pregnant, or if you are a male have you ever gotten someone pregnant?	
Yes	1.14%
No	90.63%
Does not apply[63]	8%
Do you have a teenage friend who has ever been pregnant and was not married at the time?	
Yes	44%[64]
No	56%

Earlier in this project mention was made of stress in teenager's lives. Related to stress, the following two issues; suicide and eating disorders, were found to be at a significant level of concern to teenagers in this study.

Suicide and Eating Disorders	
Have you ever considered committing suicide (killing yourself)?	
Yes	24%
No	76%
Have you ever had an eating disorder?	
Yes	15%
No	85%

When teens were asked to identify how worried they were about a number of issues they responded:

Teens Worry About…

Issue	Very Much Worried	Somewhat Worried
Violence around me	23%	55%
Being discriminated against	19%	40%
That I may take illegal drugs	13%	21%
That I will be pressured into having sex before I am ready or against my will	18%	28%
That I may have an eating disorder	8%	18%
That I might commit suicide	6%	14%
That my parents will physically hurt me	3%	9%
That I might die soon	14%	33%
That my parents will get divorced	8%	15%
That I might not get into a good college	29%	39%

---

[63] A number of teens said this did not apply simply because they were not sexually active and had not intentions to be outside of marriage.

[64] This should simply be read that 44% of the teens have a friend that has been pregnant; many of the teens could have the same friend who has been pregnant.

Church Life

Teens were asked to rate their Church participation and share their beliefs. This is what they said:

Church Life	
How would you rate your Church Attendance? I go to Church …	
More than once a week	21%
Weekly	61%
A few times a month	12%
Monthly	1%
Less than once a month	4%
I do not go to Church	0.13%
How often do you pray alone?	
Frequently	48%
Occasionally	39%
Hardly ever	9%
Never	2%
How often do you read the Bible?	
Daily	5%
Weekly	19%
Monthly	17%
Less than monthly	37%
Never	21%
Do you feel close to your Church Community?	
Yes	89%
Sometimes	0.63%
No	10%
Would you recommend your church to a friend who does not belong to another Church?	
Yes	77%
I am not sure	18%
No	4%
Do you feel comfortable in the Orthodox Church you now attend?	
Yes	94%
No	5%
How comfortable do you feel sharing your Orthodox Faith with others?	
Very comfortable	57%
Somewhat comfortable	38%
Not comfortable	3%
I will not share it	0.51%
Are you a convert to the Orthodox Church?	

Church Life	
Yes	21%
No	77%
Your View of God	
I know for sure that God exists	79%
I am mostly sure that God exists	17%
I am not sure God exists	4%
I Do not think there is a God	0.13%
I am sure there is no such thing as God	0.13%
Your View of Jesus	
I believe that Jesus is the Son of God who became a man, died on the cross for our salvation and rose from the dead	95%
Jesus was a man anointed by God to be His son	1.52%
Jesus was the Son of God, but I doubt He rose from the dead	1.39%
A great man who lived long ago	0.51%
I am not sure that Jesus really existed	0.51%
Jesus was a great prophet but not really the son of God	0.13%
Do you feel that you have a relationship with God?	
Yes	92%
Sometimes	2%
No	5%
Do you believe that there is a Heaven where people who love God and have died are with God?	
Yes	92%
Not sure there is a Heaven	6%
No	0.76%
Do you believe that there is a Hell where people who hate God and have died are in eternal punishment?	
Yes	76%
Not sure there is a Hell	19%
No	5%
My religious beliefs greatly influence how I act at school and with my friends	
Most of the time	37%
Some of the time	49%
Rarely or never	14%
How important are your religious beliefs to you?	
Very Important	72%
Fairly Important	25%
Not too important	1.77%
Not at all important	0.25%
Do you feel the Ten Commandments are relevant to your life?	
Yes	86%
Sometimes	2%

Church Life	
No	11%

Do you ever discuss your religion with your friends?

Yes	81%
No	17%

Do your friends seriously challenge what you believe in?

Yes	38%
No	61%

Do your friends ever challenge your belief in Jesus Christ?

Yes	24%
No	74%

Do you feel prepared to discuss your Orthodox Faith with your friends?

Yes	76%
No	22%

Have others asked you to join a church or religious group other than the Orthodox Church?

Yes	32%
No	68%

Teens were asked to rate how well they felt their Church helped them in several areas of life. Here is what they said:

Rate how well you feel your Church helps you - from Excellent to Poor	Excellent	Good	Okay	Fair	Poor
Learn about the Bible	39%	35%	17%	4%	3%
Learn what it means to be an Orthodox Christian	55%	29%	11%	3%	0.76%
In meeting your spiritual needs	35%	38%	19%	5%	1%
In understanding today's problems	23%	33%	27%	10%	4%
Learn about what is special about you	23%	26%	27%	4%	1%
Your religious faith grow	48%	32%	12%	12%	1%
Make friends	37%	27%	20%	7%	7%
Know adults who care about you	35%	28%	20%	10%	6%
Help other people	43%	32%	16%	5%	3%
Learn about what is right and wrong	50%	32%	12%	4%	0.51%
Learn about sex and sexual values	27%	25%	24%	11%	11%
Learn about alcohol and other drugs and what your values about them should be	22%	25%	27%	14%	10%
Have fun and good times	46%	32%	14%	3%	3%
Learn what a Christian should do about big issues such as poverty, war and loneliness	30%	29%	22%	9%	7%
Shows compassion and love to you	54%	27%	11%	5%	0.76%
As a teen to have a role in the ministry	46%	28%	15%	5%	3%

Rate how well you feel your Church helps you - from Excellent to Poor					
of the Church					

When asked if the Church responds in a meaningful way to a range of issues this is how the teens responded:

The Church responds in a meaningful way to …	Yes	No
Problems about drugs and alcohol	56%	43%
Sexual issues such as abortion and AIDs	62%	37%
Problems of marriage and divorce	73%	26%
Morality in government	37%	61%
World Problems such as war and poverty	65%	33%

Teens were asked whether a clergyman had discussed a range of issues with them, by sermon, in the classroom or other forum. This is what they said:

A clergyman has discussed with me …	Yes
Capital Punishment	28%
Cloning	24%
Abortion	59%
Pre-marital sex	64%
Birth Control	29%
Adultery	57%
Euthanasia	26%
Homosexuality	46%

Teens were asked that if they had a serious moral matter to discuss would they discuss it with each of the following people; this is what they said:

Percent of teens who said that if you had a serious moral matter to discuss they would discuss it with…	
A friend	86%
Their Pastor	52%
An aunt or uncle	42%
Another Priest besides their Pastor	40%
Youth Group Advisor or Director	36%
Another adult in your parish	32%
Teacher at school	24%
Church School Teacher	23%
A friend's parent	22%
No one	12%

Teens were asked, if they were having trouble with certain issues to whom would they turn. Here are their top answers for each issue:

If I were having trouble I would turn to…	
If I were having trouble in school I would turn to…	
Parent	60.13%
Friend my own age	19.24%
School Counselor	12.03%
Nobody	3.67%
Adult friend or relative	2.15%
Teacher	0.38%
Sibling	0.25%
If I were wondering how to handle my feelings I would turn to…	
Friend my own age	45.95%
Parent	27.85%
Nobody	9.37%
Priest	6.20%
Adult Friend or relative	4.43%
School Counselor	1.655
Church Youth Worker or Advisor	1.01%
If some of my friends started using alcohol or other drugs I would turn to…	
Parent	29.62%
Friend my own age	23.54%
Nobody	18.10%
Adult Friend or relative	10.88%
School counselor	6.84%
Priest	4.81%
Church Youth Worker or Advisor	3.04%
If I had a question about sex, I would turn to…	
Parent	39.75%
Friend my own age	29.24%
Nobody	10.63%
Adult friend or relative	8.23%
Priest	4.68%
Church Youth Worker or Advisor	2.03%
School Counselor	1.65%
On-line computer chat room	1.14%
If I were feeling guilty about something I had done, I would turn to…	
Priest	35.82%
Friend my own age	26.96%
Parent	24.30%
Nobody	5.57%
Adult Friend or relative	2.41%

Church Youth Worker or Advisor	1.27%
If I were deciding what to do with my life, I would turn to…	
Parent	67.59%
Friend my own age	8.61%
Adult friend or relative	6.08
School counselor	5.82%
Priest	4.05%
Nobody	4.05%
Church Youth Worker or Advisor	1.01%
If I were deciding whether it was right or wrong to have an abortion I would turn to…	
Parent	40.63%
Priest	28.73%
Nobody	9.75%
Friend my own age	8.10%
Adult Friend or relative	4.18%
Church Youth Worker or Advisor	2.41%
School Counselor	1.14%
I would not have an abortion	1.14%
If I were struggling with a moral or ethical issue I would turn to…	
Parent	45.57%
Priest	25.44%
Friend my own age	12.53%
Nobody	4.56%
Adult friend or relative	3.93%
Church Youth Worker or Advisor	3.29%

Cause and effect

In reviewing the data for each teen there appeared to be a correlation between certain behaviors and other behavioral outcomes. For example there was a direct correlation between how well a teen said they got along with their parents and their parents' level of discussions of issues with their teen. Teens who reported getting along very well with their parents were more likely to have discussed important issues in their lives with their parents than those who only got along fairly well. Likewise, they were significantly less likely to speak to their parents on the issues when they said that they did not get along "well at all" with their parents. The following examples are but a sampling of behaviors and or assets and deficits[65] in teen lives affecting other behaviors. While it is not in the scope of this project to explore these relationships in depth, it is the hope of this author that future work by this author and others will further explore these relationships, as they appear to be significant and profound in the outcomes of teen belief and behavior.

The following charts show the percentage of teens reporting that their parents spoke to them on the issues and how well they said they got along with their parents.

---

[65] Search Institute has done significant research on the effects of assets and deficits in the lives of teens and their direct effects on a teen's behavioral outcomes. This study supports these findings.

Parent and Teen Dialogue and their effects			
My parents **have spoken to me concerning pre-marital sexual relations** and I get Along with my Parents …		My parents **have NOT spoken to me concerning pre-marital sexual relations** and I get Along with my Parents …	
Very Well	49%	Very Well	40%
Fairly Well	47%	Fairly Well	49%
Not Very Well	4%	Not Very Well	11%
My Parents **have discussed their feeling about Birth Control** and I get Along with my Parents…		My Parents **have NOT discussed their feeling about Birth Control** and I get Along with my Parents…	
Very Well	52%	Very Well	43%
Fairly Well	44%	Fairly Well	49%
Not Very Well	4%	Not Very Well	7%
My Parents **have discussed their feeling about Abortion** and I get Along with my Parents…		My Parents **have NOT discussed their feeling about Abortion** and I get Along with my Parents…	
Very Well	52%	Very Well	39%
Fairly Well	44%	Fairly Well	52%
Not Very Well	4%	Not Very Well	9%
My Parents **have discussed their feeling about Homosexuality** and I get Along with my Parents…		My Parents **have NOT discussed their feeling about Homosexuality** and I get Along with my Parents…	
Very Well	50%	Very Well	40%
Fairly Well	45%	Fairly Well	52%
Not Very Well	5%	Not Very Well	8%
My Parents **have discussed their feeling about Aids and other sexually transmitted diseases** and I get Along with my Parents.		My Parents **have NOT discussed their feeling about Aids and other sexually transmitted diseases** and I get Along with my Parents.	
Very Well	52%	Very Well	36%
Fairly Well	43%	Fairly Well	55%
Not Very Well	4%	Not Very Well	9%
My Parents **have discussed their feeling about their expectations for my life** and I get Along with my Parents.		My Parents **have NOT discussed their feeling about their expectations for my life** and I get Along with my Parents…	
Very Well	49%	Very Well	39%
Fairly Well	45%	Fairly Well	53%
Not Very Well	5%	Not Very Well	9%
My Parents **have discussed their feeling about their expectations for my career** and I get Along with my Parents…		My Parents **have NOT discussed their feeling about their expectations for my career** and I get Along with my Parents…	
Very Well	48%	Very Well	42%
Fairly Well	47%	Fairly Well	48%
Not Very Well	5%	Not Very Well	10%

My Parents **have discussed their feeling about dating** and I get Along with my Parents…		My Parents **have NOT discussed their feeling about dating** and I get Along with my Parents…	
Very Well	48%	Very Well	40%
Fairly Well	47%	Fairly Well	51%
Not Very Well	5%	Not Very Well	9%
My Parents **have discussed their feeling about their religious faith** and I get Along with my Parents…		My Parents **have NOT discussed their feeling about their religious faith** and I get Along with my Parents…	
Very Well	48%	Very Well	40%
Fairly Well	47%	Fairly Well	48%
Not Very Well	5%	Not Very Well	12%

The fact that parents speak to their children is vital. There to be a direct correlation between whether parents have spoken with their teens on these issues and whether the teens believe that such behaviors are morally right or wrong. For example, teens who believe that abortion and other like behaviors are wrong apparently are influenced by whether or not their parents have spoken to them on the subject.

The following table consists of how teens believe and the effect discussions with their parents and clergy apparently have had on their beliefs:

Parental and Clergy effect on teens views concerning Abortion			
Concerning Abortion, only my parents	And I believe that Abortion is wrong	And I believe that Abortion is right	And I am not sure if it is right or wrong
Have spoken to me	66%	6%	25%
Concerning Abortion, only a clergyman…	And I believe that Abortion is wrong	And I believe that Abortion is right	And I am not sure if it is right or wrong
Have spoken to me	57%	4%	39%
Concerning Abortion, both my parents and a clergyman…	And I believe that Abortion is wrong	And I believe that Abortion is right	And I am not sure if it is right or wrong
Have spoken to me	79%	3%	17%
Concerning Abortion, neither my parents nor a clergyman…	And I believe that Abortion is wrong	And I believe that Abortion is right	And I am not sure if it is right or wrong
Have spoken to me	54%	8%	37%

Parental and Clergy effect on teens views concerning pre-marital sex			
Concerning pre-marital sex, only my parents	And I believe that pre-marital sex is wrong	And I believe that pre-marital sex is right	And I am not sure if it is right or wrong
Have spoken to me	61%	6%	32%
Concerning pre-marital sex, only a clergyman…	And I believe that pre-marital sex is wrong	And I believe that pre-marital sex is right	And I am not sure if it is right or wrong
Have spoken to me	63%	10%	27%
Concerning pre-marital sex,	And I believe that pre-marital sex is	And I believe that pre-marital sex is	And I am not sure if it is right or

Parental and Clergy effect on teens views concerning pre-marital sex			
both my parents and a clergyman…	wrong	right	wrong
Have spoken to me	73%	2%	23%
Concerning pre-marital sex, neither my parents nor a clergyman…	And I believe that pre-marital sex is wrong	And I believe that pre-marital sex is right	And I am not sure if it is right or wrong
Have spoken to me	63%	11%	23%

Parental and Clergy effect on teens views concerning Homosexuality			
Concerning Homosexuality, only my parents	And I believe that Homosexuality is wrong	And I believe that Homosexuality is right	And I am not sure if it is right or wrong
Have spoken to me	73%	7%	18%
Concerning Homosexuality, only a clergyman…	And I believe that Homosexuality is wrong	And I believe that Homosexuality is right	And I am not sure if it is right or wrong
Have spoken to me	66%	5%	28%
Concerning Homosexuality, both my parents and a clergyman…	And I believe that Homosexuality is wrong	And I believe that Homosexuality is right	And I am not sure if it is right or wrong
Have spoken to me	74%	5%	19%
Concerning Homosexuality, neither my parents nor a clergyman…	And I believe that Homosexuality is wrong	And I believe that Homosexuality is right	And I am not sure if it is right or wrong
Have spoken to me	59%	8%	32%

Parental and Clergy effect on teens views concerning Euthanasia			
Concerning Euthanasia, only my parents…	And I believe that Euthanasia is wrong	And I believe that Euthanasia is right	And I am not sure if it is right or wrong
Have spoken to me	49%	16%	34%
Concerning Euthanasia, only a clergyman…	And I believe that Euthanasia is wrong	And I believe that Euthanasia is right	And I am not sure if it is right or wrong
Have spoken to me	44%	24%	32%
Concerning Euthanasia, both my parents and a clergyman…	And I believe that Euthanasia is wrong	And I believe that Euthanasia is right	And I am not sure if it is right or wrong
Have spoken to me	61%	12%	27%
Concerning Euthanasia, neither my parents nor a clergyman…	And I believe that Euthanasia is wrong	And I believe that Euthanasia is right	And I am not sure if it is right or wrong
Have spoken to me	42%	20%	37%

A parent or clergyman speaking to a teen on a particular issue according to the survey, has an effect on how the teen believes compared to those teens who had neither parent or clergy speak to them. This can be seen in the following chart.

Concerning Pre-Marital Sexual Relations,	Of the 85% who believed that Pre-Marital Sex is wrong the following percent were affected by those in the left column
My Parents only spoke to me	18.5%
A Clergyman only spoke to me	15%
Both my Parents and a Clergyman spoke to me	52%
Neither spoke to me	14.5%

Sixty-five percent of teens in the survey said that they would discuss a serious moral matter with a clergyman.

Teens' willingness to discuss serious moral matters with a clergyman	
I would discuss a serious moral matter	Yes
Only with my pastor	24.5%
Only with another clergyman	12.5%
With both my pastor and another clergyman	28%

Of those who would not discuss a serious moral matter with a clergyman, another 7 percent[66] would discuss it with their youth director. According to the survey, 72 percent of the teens would be willing to turn to someone in the parish in a ministry role.

Reading the Bible also appears to have an effect on behavior. The chart below compares the 193 teens' behaviors that say they read the Bible at least weekly and the 597 teens that read the bible less than weekly or not at all.

Effects of reading the Bible on behavior			
Active in the following behavior…	Read the Bible at least Daily	Read the Bible at least Weekly	Do not read or read less than once a week
Pre-marital Sex	0.63% [67]	1.77%	7.85%
Drunk Alcohol in the past twelve months with friends	2.02%	6.08%	34.43%
Smoked cigarettes in the past month	1.14%	3.16%	20.12%
Smoked marijuana in their lifetime	0.89%	2.78%	17.21%
Very or Somewhat Worried that I might commit suicide	0.38%	2.28%	17.59%
Have considered committing suicide	0.76%	4.05%	23.92%

What teens believe also affects how they acted on that belief; the 73 teens who had responded they had pre-marital sex with someone of the opposite sex, only 28 percent

---

[66] In general 36% would go to their youth director irregardless of whether they would go to a clergyman or not

[67] Percentages in this chart are based on all 790 teens who participated in the survey.

believed that it was a wrong behavior, compared with the general teen population who did not have sexual relations where 71 percent thought it was wrong behavior. Of the 26 teens that had homosexual relations 77 percent though it was wrong behavior for them to have done so, while 87 percent of those who never had homosexual relations thought it were wrong.

One behavior affects other behaviors. Teens that drank alcohol with their friends in the past twelve months were more than 3 times more likely to have had sex than their peers who reported never having drunk alcohol in the past twelve months with their friends. However, it is not know which comes first; teens are more likely to have sex because they drink or they drink because they have had sex or even that both lead to the other behavior.

Effects of alcohol on sexual behavior	
Of the teens who reported having had sexual relations in their lifetime, the following percent reported whether they had drank alcohol at least once in the past twelve months with their friends	
Yes	77%
No	23%

Other significant parallels in one's behavior affecting other behaviors

- Of the 48 teens that reported having been forced to have sex, 41 percent reported having had sex in question 104, compared to only 9 percent in the general survey and if you exclude the 48 from the 9 percent it drops to 7 percent.
- Of those teens that reported having had sex with someone of the same sex 77 percent reported drinking alcohol in the past twelve months compared with 41 percent in the general population who drank but did not engage in homosexual behavior.
- Of the 41 teens reported to have taken illegal drugs, other than marijuana or cocaine, 85 percent of them reported also having drunk alcohol in the past twelve months.
- Those who took illegal drugs were more than twice as likely to have considered committing suicide (56%) than their peers who did not take drugs (24%).
- Of those 137 who reported having used marijuana in their lifetime, 121 (88%) also reported drinking alcohol in the past twelve months.
- Of the 41 who reported other drug use, 32 also reported having used marijuana, meaning that 78 percent of those who used other drugs also used marijuana.
- Of the 41 who reported other drug use, 37 (90%) reported having smoked cigarettes in their lifetime.
- Of the 137 teens that reported smoking marijuana 130 (95%) also reported smoking cigarettes.
- Of the 336 who reported having drunken alcohol in the past twelve months with their friends 75 percent (251) reported having smoked in their lifetime.

•Of the 375 who reported smoking in their lifetime, 251 (67%) also reported drinking alcohol with their friends, compared to the 410 who never smoked, only 83 (20%) reported having drunk alcohol in the past twelve months with their friends.

While the above comparisons are brief and limited, it is expected that similar comparisons would be found in other data comparisons from the survey, a task being left for future projects of this author and others. One should be concerned with all teen behaviors and not treat any as inconsequential, especially in light of the survey findings where one behavior appears to have influence on other behaviors. In short, one risk taking behavior tends to lead to other risk taking behaviors.

Summary of the Survey findings

While the majority of teens come from homes where both parents are Orthodox Christians, the vast majority of teens (83%) attend Church at least weekly, and eight out of ten teen's families observe the Great Lenten Fast, just over half (54%) observe the Christmas Fast, 57 percent of families say a prayer before meals, less than half of the teens pray alone on a regular basis, and less than one out of every four teens read the bible at least weekly. The survey data suggests that bible-reading frequency has a direct impact on behavioral outcomes of teens.[68] There is a similar effect to behavioral outcomes when regular prayer, fasting and Church attendance are present, particularly when a combination of two or more of these behaviors are present. Given this knowledge, effort should be placed upon further developing an active prayer, fasting and worship life of teens along with frequent bible reading habits. Consideration should also be given to the fact that teens may not regularly pray or read the bible simply because no one has taught them to do so or how to successfully approach prayer and bible reading.

Most parents spoke with their teens concerning issues such as *school grades*, *truthfulness*, *lying*, their *religious faith*, *stealing*, and *dating*, (all above 80%) while parents were less likely to have spoken to their teens concerning *pre-marital sexual relations*, *AIDS and other sexual transmitted diseases*, *fidelity in marriage*, *homosexuality*, (all under 70%) and even less when it came to issues such as abortion (59%), *birth control* (38%), and *euthanasia* (35%). Most of the issues which parents did speak to their teens were issues that parents most likely had spoken to their teens concerning since early childhood, such as telling the truth and stealing. The issues which parents were not as likely to have spoken to their teens about were the typical teen issues, which do not usually arise until the teen years, such as *pre-marital sex*, *sexually transmitted diseases*, *abortion*, and *birth control*. It was evident from the study that parents speaking to their teens on these issues did make a significant difference in what teens believed and in how they acted.[69] We need to encourage and equip parents to speak with their teens and pre-teens on these issues, so teens are better prepared and can make better decisions and more importantly so teens feel comfortable in approaching their parents when confronted with choices or problems. Even more significant is the effect of parental teen discussion was when both clergy and parents spoke with the

---

[68] See the chart *Effects of Reading the Bible on Behavior* in this chapter.
[69] See *Parents and Teen Dialogue and Their Effects* in this chapter.

teens on these issues.[70] The study suggests that we would be more successful in working with teens if parents and clergy worked together as a team.

Eighty-seven percent of teens in the survey come from homes where their birth parents are still married to each other.[71] Over 9 percent come from homes where their birth parents are divorced or separated. This means that nearly one out of every ten teens come from a single parent home or a blended family. Most Church programs assume that every child has a mother and father at home. Youth workers and pastors need to be sensitive to the fact that not every child has both parents home and or available to them. This probably also means that in ministering to teens we need to be more aware of and sensitive to the many additional issues teens from broken homes feel and face.

One third of teens arrive home from school with no adult present.[72] means that teens arrive home and have no adult supervision and are left to take care of themselves and are free to make choices of what they watch on television, view on the Internet, who they talk to on the phone, have over the house and so forth. While parents may have rules pertaining to these matters, these teens are not being supervised to see that they are following those rules. One out of every three teens appears to be unsupervised from the end of their school day until parents arrive home from work. Given this fact, youth directors might want to spend more time better equipping teens to make good decisions concerning choices of what is appropriate and what is not, particularly concerning those issues surrounding unsupervised times at home, such as the Internet, television, who they have over and what they do in the absence of adult presence. If the community geographic allows, the Church may want to look at the possibility of after school events or tutoring programs to provide safe constructive time for these teens. Consideration should also be given towards assisting parents to better equip their children to stay safe and appropriately utilize this time.

The survey indicates that the old issues of drug and alcohol abuse have not gone away. In fact, now that we know more about these issues as both health risks and gateways to other drugs and at-risk behaviors, we need to pay more attention to these issues. Over 20 percent of the teens in the survey smoked cigarettes in the past month, while 12 percent smoked cigars. Over the past twelve months 43 percent of the teens drank alcohol illegally with their friends, while 17 percent drank alcohol underage while alone. During their lifetime 18 percent smoked marijuana, another 3 percent used cocaine and nearly 6 percent used other illegal drugs. While some may view drinking alcohol and smoking cigarettes as trivial teenage behaviors, they are not. There is a significant parallel between those who drink alcohol and those who smoke cigarettes,[73] as well as those who drink and those who are sexually active.[74] We also know from other studies that the more risk taking behaviors a teen engages in, the more likely they are to engage in other risk taking behaviors.[75] working with youth should do all they can to prevent drug and alcohol abuse and to intervene when such abuse occurs.

---

[70] See *Parental and Clergy effect on teens views ...* in this chapter
[71] See *My birth parents are ...* in this chapter
[72] See *When you arrive home from school is there an adult there?* in this chapter

[73] Teens who smoked were 3 times more likely to also have gone out drinking with their friends.
[74] See *Effects of alcohol on sexual behavior* in this chapter
[75] *The Troubled Journey: A Profile of American Youth*, Search Institute, Lutheran Brotherhood, Minneapolis, MN

When asked, teens identified the following issues as their top three issues (in order of selection) confronting them on a daily basis: school grades, being liked, fears, getting along with parents, career uncertainties, peer pressures, weight problems, school problems, financing college, depression, pressure to have sex, and growing pains. Teens clearly feel a sense that they must succeed in school, be liked, know what they will do for the rest of their life, get into a good college and pay for it all. Many teens have expressed that what really matters is that they get a good education so they can make a lot of money and therefore be successful. I rarely hear a teen saying they want to get a good education so they can expand their minds, better understand themselves and those around them so they can live a fuller more meaningful life.

Depression was one of the top 10 concerns reported by teens in this survey. When we designed the survey we purposely asked teens to identify their top 3 concerns, their best friends, and then other teens their age, knowing that most of us are willing to share only so much of ourselves with others. It was interesting to see the shift in concerns as we moved to their best friends list and then their peers. For their best friend the list consisted of: School Grades, Being Liked, Getting Along with parents, Peer Pressures, School problems, Pressure to have sex, Weight Problems, Growing Pains, Depression, Financing College, Drug Abuse, and Teen Pregnancy. Here Pressure to have sex moved from 11th place on their list to 6th place on their best friends and even more significantly it moved to 4th place on their peers list. Drug Abuse, which did not even make their list, appeared 11th on their best friends list and then 3rd place on their peers list. Teen Pregnancy did not appear on their list but made it in 12th place on their best friends list and 8th on their peers list. Alcohol Abuse, which did not make their list or their best friends list was listed in 7th place on their peers list. It is interesting that alcohol abuse did not make it on their own list when 43 percent of the teens in the survey stated that they had drunk alcohol illegally in the past twelve months. This leads one to infer that either they did not see these as issues for themselves, or that it was easier to state that they were issues for others rather than themselves. The issues which made the lists, whether they were their own, their best friends or that of their peers, leads one to conclude that all of these are in fact issues they have to deal with, whether they participate in the issues themselves or are in the presence of their best friends or peers as they participate in these behaviors. In any of these cases, they are affected by these behaviors and need to be equipped to better deal with them. One of the criticisms teens gave to the Church and therefore those of us ministering to them is that we are not doing as good job as we need to in teaching them about the Church's view on these issues.[76] As Church: clergy, youth workers and parents, we need to talk to our pre-teens and teens more on these issues.

The survey strongly suggests that what teens believe directly affects what they do. Even more importantly, what they believe is directly affected by whether their parents and clergy have spoken to them on the issues.[77] When it came to issues such as abortion, pre-marital sexual relations, birth control, homosexuality, pornography, cyber sex, adultery, lying, cheating drinking, stealing, most teens did not see these behaviors as right, most saw them as wrong behaviors, though a good percent were unsure whether the behaviors were right or wrong. For example, 27 percent of teens were unsure if abortion was right or wrong.

---

[76] See *Rate how well you feel your Church helps you* ... in this chapter
[77] See *Parental and Clergy effect on teens views concerning* ... in this chapter

Additionally, the following percent of teens were unsure if the following behaviors were right or wrong: to have sex before marriage, 26 percent; to use birth control before marriage, 41 percent; homosexuality, 23 percent; pornography, 29 percent; to lie to their parents, 16 percent; to cheat on a school test, 19 percent; for them to drink a couple of beers at a party, 32 percent; capital punishment, 41 percent; and 35 percent were unsure whether euthanasia was right or wrong. While being unsure of one's position on a range of issues is not unusual during one's teen years, this clearly suggests that we need to do a better job of helping and guiding our teens to form their understanding of these issues, particularly if we as a Church want them to hold the teachings of Christ and the Church on these issues. Some of this confusion can be attributed to normal adolescent development. However, one needs to be concerned that a good deal of the confusion could also be due to the church's silence on these issues. The Church needs to better articulate Her teaching on these matters in a way that young people can grasp and incorporate into their own lives. The Church, meaning the clergy, youth workers, church school teachers, parents and other concerned adults in the Christian community, need to dialogue and teach on these issues both through their words and behavior, so young people can hear and see right behavior and thinking. Most often, despite their best efforts to the contrary, teens often reflect the adults around them in their thinking and behavior.

When it came to dating and related issues, while one third of the overall teen population in the survey had not dated in the past year, over 50 percent of all age groups from age 13-19 had dated at one time or another. Eighty-Five percent of the teens said that they had no difficulty talking to someone of the opposite sex, and 82 percent of the teens said that they think of sex at least some of the time and this included both males and females. When asked if they ever had sexual intercourse nearly 10 percent said that they had. The percent of teens who said they had sexual intercourse were equally both male and female and were as young as age 13 for both males and females. Some 13 year olds reported having had sexual intercourse six or more times. A similar situation existed when it came to homosexual behavior where 3 percent of teens said they had sex with someone of the same sex as they, and those who were homosexually active were as young as age 13 and again both male and female. It is clear from the findings that age 13 is not too young to begin talking about issues surrounding sexuality. What we do not know from the survey is whether children younger than age 13 are sexually active. One might assume that pre-teens are sexually active, given the number of 13 year olds dating and having both heterosexual and homosexual relationships. This survey was conducted with teens starting at age 13. These results indicate that we might want to find out what is happening in the pre-teen years and these results further indicate that the pre-teen years may not be too early to begin teaching right moral behavior. Again, as a Church, we need to better communicate the Church's teaching on these issues and as early as the pre-teen years.[78]

One out of every four teens in the survey has considered committing suicide, while 15 percent have had an eating disorder. Teens in general were somewhat or very worried, that they might not get into a good college, about the violence around them, being discriminated against, that they would be pressured into having sex before they were ready or against their will, that they might die soon, that they might take illegal drugs, that they might have an

---

[78] Just over 50% of teens said that the Church was doing a good or excellent job in teaching about sexual values.

eating disorder, that their parent's might get divorced, and that they might commit suicide. These are not casual issues for teens to deal with alone. Adults need to be more aware of the pressures confronting teens, aware of the danger signs and more active in listening and dialoguing with teens. More time needs to be spent with teens letting them know that we as adults hear their concerns, understand them and are ready to help them work through these issues and fears. One of the most frightening things to teens is that that they feel at times that they are the only ones going through these issues, or that they are not normal because they have these feelings and concerns. We need to assure them that they are not alone, that many of the feelings they have are normal, and that they can successfully work through these issues. At times, we may even need to be there to help and show them how to work through these issues. With a third of the teens arriving home from school with no adult present, one can assume that teens are often left to work through many of these issues alone. We clearly want to change this and bring more adults that are appropriate into the lives of our teens who can be there to assist both the teens and their parents.

Eighty-two percent of the teens attended Church Services at least once a week. Ninety-five percent of teens held the Orthodox Christian view that Jesus was the Son of God who became a man, died on the cross for our salvation and rose from the dead. Ninety-two percent of teens felt they had a relationship with God, while the same percent believed that there was a Heaven where people who loved God and have died are with God. Eighty-six percent of teens felt the Ten Commandments were relevant to their life. Ninety-four percent of teens felt comfortable with the Orthodox Church they were currently attending and 95 percent felt at least somewhat comfortable sharing their faith with others.

While teens in general were able to "give" back the Orthodox teachings, when it came to living these beliefs out the results were less positive. It appears that the Church Schools are doing their job in teaching the information to teens. What now needs to happen is that we need to help make the connection between what is being taught in the classroom and what is lived out in life. For example: only 37 percent stated that their religious beliefs greatly influenced how they acted at school most of the time. Another 49 percent said that their beliefs greatly influenced how they acted at school with their friends some of the time. Forty-eight percent frequently pray and only 5 percent read the bible daily and another 19 percent read the bible weekly. One out of every four teens does not feel prepared to discuss their faith with friends. When it came to the things they do, such as smoking and drinking many of teens do not appear to be affected by the Church's teaching on these matters.

Part of the reason for the Church's failure to affect how teens act on a daily basis may have to do with the quality of the job teens perceive the Church is doing in teaching them about the values concerning these behaviors. For example, the following percentages said the Church was doing an excellent job in the following areas: "The Church helps you"— learn about the bible, 39 percent; learn what it means to be an Orthodox Christian, 55 percent; meet your spiritual needs, 35 percent; understanding today's problems, 23 percent; learn about what is special about you, 23 percent; (help your) religious faith grow, 48 percent; make new friends, 37 percent; learn about what is right and wrong, 50 percent; learn about sex and sexual values, 27 percent; learn about alcohol and other drugs and what your values about them should be, 22 percent; learn about what a Christian should do about the big issues such as poverty, war and loneliness, 30 percent. When asked if the Church responds in a meaningful way to the following issues the following percent of teens said yes:

problems about drugs and alcohol, 56 percent; sexual issues such as abortion and AIDS, 62 percent; problems of marriage and divorce, 73 percent; morality in government, 37 percent; world problems such as war and poverty, 65 percent. When teens were asked if a clergyman had discussed certain issues with them, the following percent said yes: capital punishment, 28 percent; cloning, 24 percent; abortion, 59 percent; pre-marital sex 64 percent; birth control, 29 percent; adultery, 57 percent; euthanasia, 26 percent; homosexuality, 46 percent.

From the data received in the survey it appears that teens perceive we could do a better job. One of the ways in which we can better develop the connection between what teens are learning in the classroom and how they are living it out in their daily life is to have more interaction and dialogue on these issues between teens, parents and clergy. Teens may not hold the Church's view on many issues because they simply do not know what the Church teaches or do not know how to incorporate it into their daily life. It may also be the case that their behaviors do not match Church teachings because they have not been empowered and enabled to live out the Gospel message. Time would be well spent in interactive dialogue and case studies with teens on real issues that they deal with on a daily basis, so they can be better informed on the issues and have literally practiced healthy responses to the issues confronting them in life. While this may not be the job of church schools, one would certainly think it is the job of youth ministry. Youth ministry is where the connection between what is taught in the classroom and how it is lived out is made. It is the youth worker's job to help make the teachings of the Church come to life for the teen and for it to have impact in a meaningful and real way that teens can grasp and understand.

We know from comparison of the data that parents and clergy also play a very important role in making this connection occur.[79] Communities would do well to build a youth ministry team consisting of teens, parents, clergy, and youth workers, all working towards the same goal of enabling young people to live out the faith and make good choices. One of the most encouraging pieces of information to come out of the survey is that teens said they would go to their pastor, 52 percent; another clergyman besides their pastor, 40 percent; a youth group advisor or director, 36 percent, if they had a serious moral matter to discuss. One of the goals of youth ministry should be to increase the number of teens who would go to a Church leader to seek help. It is the belief of this author that this would happen much more often if we as a Church more openly addressed these issues and let the teens know that it is acceptable for them to speak to Church leaders and teachers on these matters. It is striking to see the change in questions when leading a teen workshop when the leader tells the teens it is acceptable to ask questions on any issue affecting them in their daily life. It is even more striking to see the openness of that dialogue when teens know that they are being taken seriously and that their questions are honestly being answered with love and concern for their welfare.

Two groups of people came up in the survey as people whom teens would most likely turn to for help with certain issues: their friends and their parents. We can accomplish much if we also train parents and teens to help respond to teens' questions and concerns. Parents more than anyone want the best for their own children. It is good and right that teens go to their parents for advice and help. We should encourage this to occur more often. We can better equip parents to handle the questions and concerns of their teens, to be more aware of

---

[79] See Parent and Teen Dialogue and their effects, as well as Parental and clergy effect on teens views concerning … in this chapter.

the issues confronting their children, and to create a forum where parents can share ideas and concerns. We may even want to create the opportunity for parents and the Church to jointly work on issues affecting our children in the schools and community. We would do well to help parents find support within the Church community with people that say and do that which is morally right concerning their children.

Teens often turn to other teens for answers. At times this is very frightening given the fact that the peers they turn to often have no more or better answers than the person asking the question. I often equate some teens asking other teens for help in making good moral choices with a drowning person asking another drowning person to save them. However, the reality is that we may never convince teens to always go to other adults for guidance and help, perhaps because adults are not always available, or because teens may perceive they do not understand. What we can do though, is to better equip teens to make good choices for themselves and consequently give better advice to their peers through their own advice and actions. We also want to work towards opening channels of communications between teens and adults, so teens know that there are adults standing there ready to assist when necessary.

While some teens may perceive that the Church is not doing the very best job She can, and She may not be, and that parents do not speak to teens as often as they should on the issues, the good news is that there appears to be a great value and a direct impact from the positive adult influence teens have in their lives. It is real adult people that seem to effect change in teen's lives and influences what they think, and not simply the media, the schools, their peers and other influences around them. Our emphasis ought to be on building healthy thriving adult and teen relationships with and for our teens, so that they will be better equipped to navigate their way through life.

CHAPTER 4
AN OVERVIEW OF THE TEACHINGS OF THE ORTHODOX CHURCH

- Abortion
- Birth Control
- Pre-Marital Sex
- Homosexuality
- Alcohol and Drug Abuse
- Euthanasia

The Orthodox Teen Survey raised many issues for which the Church needs to articulate Her position in an understandable and easily accessible form for the general Orthodox and non-Orthodox population. By covering the topics listed above the author hopes to give a general feeling of the Church's approach and basis for many of the Church's teachings on moral and ethical issues, as well as to how an Orthodox youth worker and or pastor might approach these subjects with teens. It is hoped that by covering these topics, that the reader will be able to better understand the mind of the Church and move from these topics to others with a basic understanding of the Church's approach. It is also hoped that *The Orthodox Teen Survey* and this chapter will encourage others to explore, write, dialogue, and teach on the many issues raised in this survey. The purpose here is not to do battle with those who oppose the views of the Church; rather it is to guide those who have a deep love of God, His Church and those in the Christian Community. It is the intent of this author to begin to present the subject to the reader as a way of guiding them to live a life rooted in Christ and His teachings. The view of the Church is that living the life given by God leads to *Life* here and now on earth and in the Kingdom. It remains the goal of every Christian to be in communion with God here and now, and to spend eternal paradise with God our Creator. It is the belief of this author that living the life of the Scriptures in the Church, gives us the best possible opportunity to enjoy our time now and to spend eternity in Paradise with God. The ultimate goal of this study is that both the young and older members of the Christian Community will better understand their faith, their relationship with God and their relationship and responsibilities with one another.

In light of the survey results, one of the main objectives in youth ministry should be to strengthen those teens that already believe in Christ and do what the Church teaches in relation to the issues. Likewise we want to change the minds and behavior of those who think and do differently than what the Church teaches, and to assist those who are unsure of what is right and wrong, so as to enable them to come to an appropriate understanding of these issues through the eyes of the Church and to act appropriately. Ultimately by bringing about this change, we will help teens live a better, healthier and Christ centered life, in a manner that brings joy, peace, happiness and health.

Abortion

Given the divisiveness that this issue causes on contemporary North Americans', it is not surprising that teens would be unsure what they should believe in regards to abortion. Further compounding this problem is the seeming silence of the Church on this issue. While the Church has a clear and strong position on the issue of abortion, in recent years the Church has not taken an active part in the public debate and discussion of this issue. Abortion also is not part of the formal church school curriculum, or other formal teen and adult discussion forums on the parish level. The Church has not been silent because she does not care, but because many in the church feel the Church's position is well known. It is apparent from the survey that whether it is or is not well know, many teens are unsure what they should believe concerning abortion.

In the survey, teens were asked in three different ways what they believed concerning abortion. They were first asked, "Is it right or wrong to have an abortion for reasons other than to save the life of the mother?" to which 67 percent said it was wrong, only 5 percent said it was right and 27 percent were unsure. They were then asked, "Is it right or wrong to have an abortion to save the physical life of the mother?" to this question 38 percent saw it as right, which is the one occasion upon which the Church understands the possible need for a couple to choose to have an abortion, 20 percent saw it as wrong and 41 percent were unsure if it was right or wrong. Teens were then asked, "Is it right or wrong to have an abortion for any reason?" less than 3 percent thought it was right, 63 percent thought it was wrong and 33 percent were unsure if it was right or wrong. It was clear from the survey that while a slim majority saw abortion as wrong, in all three scenarios, at least 3 out of 10 teens were not sure whether having an abortion was right or wrong. Abortion is one of those issues on which teens receive many mixed and conflicting messages.

Youth workers need to help teens discern what they believe on this issue and to help teens come to an understanding of what and why the Church holds the position she does on abortion. While lecturing or sermonizing may appear to be the best way to convey this information it is often ineffective in assisting the teen to incorporate this belief into his or her own belief system. It is often more beneficial to allow teens to enter into a free dialogue on this issue. One of the goals of that dialogue is to help teens see that the Church views all life as precious and that when we devalue anyone's life no matter how early in development or how late in late in life, we devalue and dehumanize all life.

We know from the survey that one of the most effective ways of teens understanding and accepting the Church's teaching on abortion is for both parents and clergy to dialogue with them on this issue.[80]   of the strategy of having parents and clergy work together on this issue ought to involve spending time with the parents, so they better understand the Church's teaching on abortion and can better articulate it to their children. Providing the opportunity in youth group and at retreats for teens to dialogue on this issue also provides opportunities for teens to articulate and better understand their own position on abortion. I have found it helpful at retreats to provide a group of teens with materials on the Church

---

[80] See *Parental and Clergy effect on teens views concerning Abortion* in Chapter 3

position on abortion (a sample of which is provided below) or any other issue for that matter and ask them to study the material (20 minutes or more) and then have them present the Church's teaching on this subject to their peers. I find at least two things happen through this process: first teens take the task seriously when they know they will be getting up in front of their peers and secondly both they and their peers listen more intently to the material. I have found that simply exposing them to the teaching of the Church in a non-threatening open dialogue allows them to better understand the Church's position. In hearing the Church's position, which is very logical and loving, most teens are ready to accept it. I believe that most teens want to do that which is right; they simply need to hear and be taught what is right and what is wrong. Teens are ready to accept and incorporate the truth into their lives, but they need to hear the message and be allowed to freely discuss, debate and then own this truth.

The following material on abortion is an example of material that I would give to both teens and adults in preparing them to discuss the issue of abortion. I do not feel a need to give them views opposing that of the Church as I feel they already have been inundated with that material. Further, my intent here is to convey to them the Church's teaching on abortion. When I ask teens to give a presentation on the material, I specifically ask them to present the Church's teaching, not their own or anything else that they have already learned elsewhere. This is important because they need to clearly hear the Church's teaching so they can place their personal beliefs on this issue along with other views alongside that of the Church. In seeing these positions side by side the logical discerning teen will easily see the Church's teaching as the only logical option, though I want them to come to that conclusion through their own thought process. Again, the purpose here is not simply that the teens accept the Church's view as their own, but that they accept and incorporate all of the issues surrounding the teaching; that killing is wrong, that all life is precious, that God loves all of us, that God is the source of life, that procreation is participation in the life creating action of God, and so forth.

The Church's view on Abortion

The Church teaches that God is the source and sustainer of life and that He created us as male and female with a purpose in mind. The Church views sexual relations between a husband and wife as something very sacred and good and, in fact, when it bears life, the Church views this action as participating in the very action of God's Creation. The Scriptures say that God became man so that we might become one with Him. Here in this very action of sexual intercourse, when it bears fruit and a child is conceived we already have a foretaste of becoming one with God, by sharing in the creative life giving action of generating life. "For in sexual intercourse, it is not only the seeds of physical being that are united, but also a soul. A father and mother not only transmit their physical characteristics to the child, but they also transmit its soul. This sacred power man possesses of continuing God's creation with Him is indeed a great wonder."[81] Hence, to generate life is participation in the Divine Life. The Church opposes abortion, because abortion consciously stops the process of life already begun. God is the source of life. Once the woman's egg is fertilized;

---

[81] Rev. Fr. John Kowalczyk, *An Orthodox View of Abortion* (Minneapolis, Minnesota: Gopher State Litho Company, 1977), 6-7

if this fertilized egg is allowed to grow and develop in the woman's womb, it will result in the birth of a child. Therefore any intervention in the development of the fertilized egg, at any point once that process has begun (conception), results in the ending of life and a rejection of the wonderful gift of life and the ability to generate life given to us by God. Hence, it is not only a rejection of the gift of a new life, but rebellion against God's creative energy and love.

Abortion is not a new controversy brought about by new technologies and understandings of our body. Abortion is an ageless controversy struggled with and recorded at least from the time of Hippocrates, the ancient Greek "father of medicine." Until recently, doctors who took the Oath of Hippocrates[82] swore not to give poisonous drinks that would abort a fetus. In Roman law abortion was considered a major crime and in the New Testament a fetus was considered a life already begun. The New Testament Gospel written by the physician Luke has as its beginning, the conception of two children. The first, John the Baptist, the one called to prepare the way of the Lord and the second, the Christ Child, the Messiah, God Incarnate. We read in Luke the account of these two conceptions:

> In the sixth month the angel Gabriel was sent from God to a city of Galilee named Nazareth, to a virgin betrothed to a man whose name was Joseph, of the house of David; and the virgin's name was Mary. And he came to her and said, "Hail, O favored one, the Lord is with you!" But she was greatly troubled at the saying, and considered in her mind what sort of greeting this might be. And the angel said to her, "Do not be afraid, Mary, for you have found favor with God. And behold, you will conceive in your womb and bear a son, and you shall call his name Jesus.
>
> > He will be great, and will be called the Son of the Most High;
> > and the Lord God will give to him the throne of his father David,
> > and he will reign over the house of Jacob for ever;
> > and of his kingdom there will be no end."
>
> And Mary said to the angel, "How shall this be, since I have no husband?" And the angel said to her,
>
> > "The Holy Spirit will come upon you,
> > and the power of the Most High will overshadow you;
> > therefore the child to be born will be called holy, the Son of God.
>
> And behold, your kinswoman Elizabeth in her old age has also conceived a son; and this is the sixth month with her who was called barren. For with God nothing will be impossible." And Mary said, "Behold, I am the handmaid of the Lord; let it be to me according to your word." And the angel departed from her.
> In those days Mary arose and went with haste into the hill country, to a city of Judah, and she entered the house of Zechariah and greeted Elizabeth. And when Elizabeth heard the greeting of Mary, the babe leaped in her womb; and Elizabeth was filled with the Holy Spirit and she exclaimed with a loud cry, "Blessed are you among women, and blessed is the fruit of your womb! And why is this granted me, which the mother of my Lord should come to me? For behold, when the voice of your greeting came to my ears, the babe in my womb leaped for joy. And blessed is she who believed that there would be a fulfillment of what was spoken to her from the Lord." (Luke 1:26-46)

---

[82] See the appendix for the text of the Hippocratic Oaths from the 5th century BC and the present.

Likewise, the Church in Her liturgical life recognizes these two conceptions by setting aside feast days nine months before the Church celebrates each of these births. For example, in the case of Jesus Christ, while the Church celebrates His birth on December 25th, she also celebrates His conception on March 25th; In the case of Mary the Church celebrates Her birth on September 8th and Her conception on December 9th; in the case of John the Baptist his birth on June 24th and his conception on September 23rd. Both the scriptural accounts and the liturgical calendar make a statement concerning the Church's belief that life begins at conception. In the case of our Lord, March 25th is one of the major Feast Days of the year. The Church believes it is at the moment of conception life has been given and begins; She marks these days with great celebration and sacredness. In the great feast of the Nativity of Mary (September 8th) celebrated as the first feast of the Church New Year (which begins on September 1st) one reads concerning Mary, that she was chosen by God before she was even conceived: "Come, all ye believers, let us hasten to the Virgin; for behold she was forechosen a Mother to our God before she was conceived in the womb…"[83] It appears that even before conception God has plans for our life.

In keeping with the scriptural teachings the Apostles spoke out against abortion, "Do not murder; do not commit adultery; do not corrupt boys; do not go in for sorcery; do not murder a child by abortion or kill a new-born infant."[84] , one of the early Church writers, said, "You shall love your neighbor more than your own life. You shall not slay the child by abortion. You shall not kill that which has already been generated." (Epistle of Barnabas XIX, 5) St. Basil writes, "Those who give potions for the destruction of the child conceived in the womb are murderers, as are those who take potions which kill the child." (Letters, CLXXXVIII, Canon 8) St. John Chrysostom considered the abortionist as "even worse than a murderer." (Homilies in Romans, XXIV) St. Gregory of Nyssa writes: "There is no question about that which is bred in the uterus, both growing and moving from place to place. It remains, therefore that we must think that the point of commencement of existence is one and the same for body and soul." (On the Soul and the Resurrection - Gregory of Nyssa) Modern Orthodox theologians continue with the thought pattern found in the writings of the Fathers. John Meyendorff, writes, "The fact that this interruption takes place makes, of course, a psychological difference, but does not change the nature of the act of abortion being killing, and as such a very grave sin. Because killing is evil …" ("The Orthodox Church" [Newspaper] October 1972). Again, "… human life begins at the moment of conception and all who hold life as sacred and worthy of preservation whenever possible are obliged at all costs to defend the lives of unborn children regardless of the stage of their embryonic development." ("Seminar in Medical Ethics," St. Vladimir's Theological Quarterly, Vol. 17, no 3, 1973, p. 246.)

Stanley Harakas, one-time professor of Ethics and Morality at Hellenic College and Holy Cross Orthodox School of Theology, writes in his book *Contemporary Moral Issues*:

> One of the most common arguments used by supporters of abortion on demand is that a woman's right to privacy extends to control over what happens within her own body,

---

[83] From the Aposticha of Vespers of the Fest of the Birth of the Theotokos, September 8, by the hymnographer Sergius, as found in the The Divine Prayers and Services of the Antiochian Orthodox Christian Archdiocese of North America. p. 287

[84] Didache, Teachings of the Apostles II,2

including the contents of her uterus. This argument was accepted by the Supreme Court (as far as the first three months of pregnancy are concerned) in its 1973 decision on abortion. Some advocates of this position go so far as to refer to the nascent life as a cancerous growth, or "piece of extraneous tissue", that has invaded the mother's womb. Orthodoxy rejects such notions due to the great value attached to life by God, and the fact that life is a gift which no person has the right to take. If we do not have the right to take our own lives, how much more so must it be that we have no right to take the innocent life of the embryo or fetus in the womb? If our bodies are "temples of the Holy Spirit" as we profess, then to kill an innocent human being is a crime, not only against that person, but also against the Holy Spirit. That the developing persons inside the mother's womb has a life separate from its mother is evident from the fact that its chromosomal makeup is different from the mother's since it is a combination drawn from both mother and father. Further, it is genetically unique; its particular combination of traits and characteristics shall never be repeated.

Further he writes;

A second argument commonly made by those who favor abortion "rights" is that, particularly if the removal of the nascent life occurs during the first few weeks of pregnancy, no human person, or person who is "fully human" has been destroyed. They also claim that unwanted children will not have the opportunity of developing into "responsible personhood," or will jeopardize the "personhood" of parents and siblings, due to the added burden they impose. In opposition, we profess that no human being is ever fully a "person", but that all persons have the potential to become "fully human", to achieve union with God. Therefore, we cannot declare on the basis of "personhood" that the fetus in the womb has no value, or lesser value in the eyes of both God and man than a person born.

Further supporting Fr. Harakas' statements are the effects that new medical technology is having upon the abortion rights movement. This new technology supports the fact that the fetus is not a "piece of extraneous tissue", but a visible child in formation:

Faye Wattleton, former head of Planned Parenthood, was crushed to learn that women's attitudes on abortion are not what she supposed they were. A poll conducted by Wattleton's new group, the Center for Gender Equality found that 53 percent of American women think abortion should be allowed only after rape or incest, to save a woman's life, or not at all. Only 28 percent said abortion should be generally available, and 70 percent want more restrictions.

Another sign of slippage in support for abortion shows up in UCLA's annual national survey of the attitudes of college freshmen. Support for legal abortion dropped for the sixth straight year. In 1990 it was 64.9 percent. Now it is a bare majority, 50.9 percent. The National Opinion Research Center in Chicago found declining opposition to legal abortion from 1988 to 1996. But opposition climbed again in 1998 and is now in the 55 percent range.

Declining support for abortion owes something to the gruesome details that emerged in the debate over "partial-birth" abortion. Improvements in ultrasound imaging also tend to undermine abortion, cutting through the abstractions of "choice" and "reproductive rights" and showing pregnant women how much a fetus resembles a newborn. When ultrasound video shows the fetus in 3-D, support for abortion could drop further.[85]

Aside from the theological and technological arguments, are the inherent human emotions surrounding the tragedy of abortion. One common comment heard by this author from young women who have chosen to have an abortion is that they were encouraged or

---

[85] John Leo, "The Joy of Sexual Values," *U.S. News and World Report,* 1 March 1999, 13.

strongly convinced to have an abortion. Often these women had been encouraged to seek abortion as a solution by their own parents or other relatives, friends, teachers and advisors. The tragedy is that often this council is misguided and the young woman never really comes to terms with her own feelings on this issue until it is too late and she recognizes that she has ended a life—a life conceived and carried in her own womb, a life given and taken by her own choice. A similar comment appears in the February 5, 1999 Greek Orthodox Observer Newspaper,[86]

> While researching her book, Real Choices: Listening to Women, Looking for Alternatives to Abortion, writer Frederica Mathews-Green came across a recurring theme. "As I traveled the country holding 'listening groups' with women who had abortions, I always asked, 'What situation caused you to make this decision?' I expected to hear tales of financial woe, yet nearly 90 percent of the women told me they had had their abortion because of a relationship—because someone they loved, a boyfriend or a parent, told them to. When asked what anyone could have done to help them complete the pregnancy, over and over the answer was: Just stand by me. "If only I had one person to stand by me." Writes Mrs. Mathews Green.[87]

Many teens, including teens participating in the Orthodox Teen Study, are either unaware or confused about the teachings of the Church on abortion or have chosen to believe otherwise. When it comes to deciding how one believes on this issue, relationships really do matter. Many of our teens that believe abortion is wrong, aside from their intrinsic human emotions do so because they have been guided and nurtured by others who believe the same. It is not unexpected that one out of every four teens are unsure if abortion is right or wrong, even when allowing it in the case of a mother's life being at stake.[88] Young people, even at very young ages, are presented with abortion as an acceptable and legal solution to a pregnancy crisis and a right to be had upon demand, even without parental consent in the case of minors. They hear of the ease of obtaining an abortion but seldom of the physical, emotional, and spiritual pain and suffering, let alone of the suffering and the end of life for the child. It is the hope of this author that more qualified, loving adults will stand by young people and share with them just how precious life is and that even when serious mistakes or sins, like pre-marital sex take place, resulting in pregnancy, the life created is still precious and belongs to God. Although this intercourse may take place outside of marriage without the blessings of God (hence sinful), the creation of life is still

---

[86] This quote appeared in an article concerning an Orthodox Movement entitled "ZOE for Life!" which is a pregnancy outreach for women and exists to help young unmarried women who have chosen to bring their child to full term. It is a movement to help young women complete their pregnancy and either keep their child or place the child with an adoptive family. *ZOE for Life* can be reached at 1-440-893-9990.

[87] Eleni Daniels, "Zoe for Life! Crisis Pregnancy Outreach for Women," *The Orthodox Observer*, (New York: Greek Orthodox Archdiocese of N. America), 5 February, 1999, 7.

[88] As mentioned earlier, the one case when the church understands a couple's decision to have an abortion is when a choice needs to be made concerning saving the physical life of the mother when the alternative is that mother and/or child will die if there is no intervention. This is not saying in this instance this is not killing. The Church still recognizes that the choice is made to *kill* the child in the womb, but the decision is understood when, if no action is taken, both or at least the mother will die. It is here, in consultation with their spiritual father that the couple makes the decision to save the mother's life, leaving it to the mercy of God and praying for restoration of health and soul, well aware of the sacrifice being made to save a life. Again, the emphasis is on saving and preserving life as best one can. Typically the choice is without intervention both will die. It is not considered an affront to God to try and save at least one of those lives. Though even and perhaps especially here the mother and father will still bear the loss of a child and all that surrounds that real loss.

participation in the divine creative action of God. Choosing an abortion is not taking responsibility for a choice to participate in God's creative action and further compounds the first sin and effectively leads to the death of part of oneself and certainly of the life created.

Married couples at times are confronted with increasing pressure from doctors to conduct prenatal tests, which sometimes leads to recommendations of aborting children whose tests show that the child may be born with physical or psychological defects. Here again, Harakas' words, that none of us are *fully human* nor will reach our full human potential until we see God in His Kingdom, gives a good indication as to where the Church stands on this issue. One might ask, who are we to determine what constitutes a full human being and that even a child born with physical or mental challenges, no matter how severe, is still capable of seeing, feeling and participating in God's majestic beauty of creation and His presence, albeit maybe differently than we may think and perceive, none-the-less as capable and maybe even more free to enjoy God's presence. Another difficult area for many to accept is the case in which a rape results in a pregnancy. The Orthodox Church's position is that even in the unfortunate and uncontrollable instance of rape, abortion is not a solution. Here perhaps is one of the most difficult choices a young woman may be called to make, when she has been violated, to carry the violator's baby to term. Perhaps this is where she can take control and choose good over evil, choose to give life rather than destroy and unlike her perpetrator, grant life and joy if not to herself in keeping the child, then in offering the child to a loving couple through adoption. Parents, who have been violated by their child being violated in instances of rape or incest, often want the solution that seems to offer the quickest solution for the child and all involved. Choosing abortion, while it may seem to be the quickest of choices, in fact itself leaves many more scars for the person already victimized. The author is very mindful of the violation that has taken place, and offers the wisdom of the Church as a possible means to real healing. It is the belief of this author that the person violated by rape or incest, is again violated through abortion and that by carrying and bearing the child and offering the child up for adoption to a loving couple itself can very well be a source of healing and strength at this most difficult time. In any of the instances above, the choice to abort or not to abort has much to do with those surrounding the young person and what they counsel and support. Fr. John Kowalczk reminds all of us surrounding those dealing with a crisis pregnancy:

> Any involvement in an abortion; having one, performing one, condoning one, is an action against God. Abortion can be termed a hostile act of rebellion against God's very work of creation. And do not the words "hostile rebellion against God" sum up the very essence of the work of Satan?[89]

Birth Control

The survey indicates that many teens display confusion between the use of birth control prior to marriage and its connection to pre-marital sex. While 68 percent of teens said it was wrong to have sex before marriage, less than 40 percent said it was wrong to use birth control before marriage. Nearly 41 percent of teens were unsure if the use of birth control was right or wrong before marriage compared to nearly 26 percent who were unsure if it was

---

[89] An Orthodox View of Abortion, Rev. Fr. John Kowalczyk, p. 7

right or wrong to have sex before marriage. While less than 6 percent of teens thought it was right to have sex prior to marriage over 18 percent thought it was right to use birth control prior to marriage. The data concerning birth control use and pre-marital sex do not match one another, when one would expect them to match. In discussions with teens on this issue, as a follow-up to the survey, two types of comments were made that leads one towards possibly understanding this confusion. Most teens responded by saying, "but using birth control is the responsible thing to do if you are going to have sex" and a small number of females mentioned that there are other medical uses of birth control besides preventing pregnancy. The most common of the responses as I interviewed teens across North America was that "using birth control was the responsible and right thing to do." I was stuck by the implication that using birth control before marriage was a responsible thing, despite the overwhelming number of teens who were able to understand that sex prior to marriage was wrong. Perhaps President George W Bush's emphasis on abstinence from sex for teens, may raise the awareness of virginity as a legitimate American way of life.

In further discussions with teens on the issue of birth control, teens expressed that they hear the message so often on having "safe sex" that they begin to think they are supposed to have sex, as long as it is "safe sex." In fact teens, both male and female, over the last several years have approached me feeling that something was wrong with them, because they were not having sex, while everyone else was having sex. When I asked them why they thought everyone was having sex, they typically responded that that was the message they felt they were getting when taught about "safe sex." Teens typically received the message on "safe sex" as, "we know you are going to have sex, so be smart and have safe sex." Being sexually active during one's teen years and outside of marriage is further implied and expressed to teens as normal and acceptable by the frequency of shows which openly display or imply sex outside of marriage, particularly on television programs targeted towards teens.

The confusing messages teens receive concerning "safe sex" may be why so many teens would see using birth control prior to marriage as the right thing to do. It needs to be conveyed to teens that just because they may follow the instructions of having "safe sex" this does not mean that having sex prior to marriage is therefore acceptable or the right thing to do. From the survey, one senses that teens understand that sex outside of marriage is wrong; but that they are unable to make the connection that having "safe sex" is still having sex outside of marriage. We need to clarify the issue that the only "safe sex" is sex between two virgins who marry one another and remain faithful to each other. The "safe sex" message used in society today implies that there is only a physical dimension to sex and no spiritual and emotional dimension, which often are the greatest expression of sexuality. Teens need to know that using birth control and condoms may provide for safer physical sex, (though there are no guarantees) but that sex outside of marriage whether they use birth control or not, still carries with it emotional and spiritual issues that they will deal with for the rest of their life. The emotional and spiritual issues will be covered in more depth in the section on pre-marital sex. The following section will illuminate the consensus of many Orthodox Theologians on the acceptable use of birth control within marriage. In condemning the use of birth control outside of marriage, one needs to be careful that teens do not perceive that birth control within marriage is also always condemned. Too often teens hear what we have to say concerning sex and perceive that the Church sees sex in all instances as "bad." It is important that teens understand that within marriage the Church sees a sexual relation between husband and wife as good and even necessary to a healthy marriage and that birth control may be part of that healthy expression. It is also felt that in teaching teens what not to do, in regard to birth control, we also need to teach them the Church's understanding of appropriate sexual relations. We need to do this so they better understand that birth control has an appropriate use and so that they are not confused when they learn or hear later in life of this appropriate use and place within marriage. Our purpose here is not to condemn birth control itself, but its inappropriate use in fostering pre-marital or extramarital sexual relations. The following is presented as what one might want to convey to teens concerning the appropriate use of birth control.

The Church's view on Birth Control

It should be noted from the outset that there is no direct Orthodox Teaching on this issue in the Scriptures, Canons of the Church or Early Church Fathers. There is however, a consensus amongst some modern theologians on this issue. It is that consensus which this author will draw upon in this section dealing with Birth Control. It should also be noted that this author and the theologians cited here consider birth control as preventing fertilization of the female egg and not the expulsion of the fertilized egg by means of preventing implantation in the uterus. Hence means of birth control might mean medication that mimics the female cycle, so an egg does not drop down the female fallopian tube into the uterus where it can be fertilized. Condoms, following the female cycle and having sex only when the woman is most likely not to get pregnant and the like would be acceptable. What would not be considered birth control would be usage of an *I.U.D.*, Medication (such as the RU-486 pill) or the like which prevents implantation or expels a fertilized egg. In short, what prevents fertilization (conception) is considered birth control, what ends the potential life after conception, no matter how early, is considered abortion. In the following, the author refers only to birth control with the added understanding of birth control only within marriage. The issue of birth control outside of marriage will be covered under the section on pre-marital sexual relations.

John Meyendorff, the eminent Orthodox theologian and Professor of Patristic Theology at St. Vladimir's Seminary from 1959-1992, taught that the Orthodox Church has never endorsed straight condemnation of birth control within marriage, providing that birth control is not used as a means to never have children. Some Orthodox theologians teach that a couple may initially, when married, choose to wait to have children for a short time and again after they have had a sufficient number of children choose to have no more, as a means of appropriately caring for their children and administering the affairs of their household. However, Meyendorff also taught that for the Orthodox Christian couple choosing to never have children or carelessly waiting too long to have children are unacceptable options, given the importance of bearing and raising children as a necessary out-flow of the couples love for one another. Children are the natural outcome of a married couple's love, with the only exception being the couple's possible inability to conceive and bear children. Meyendorff writes:

> In fact, childbirth and raising of children are indeed a great joy and God's blessing.
> There can be no Christian marriage without an immediate and impatient desire of both

parents to receive and share in this joy. A marriage where children are unwelcome is founded upon defective, egotistic and fleshly form of love. In giving life to others, man imitates God's creative act and, if he refuses to do so, he not only rejects his Creator, but also distorts his own humanity; for there is no humanity without an "image and likeness of God," i.e., without a conscious, or unconscious desire to be a true imitator of the life-creating Father of all.[90]

Further expounding on this issue, Fr. Stanley Harakas writes:

> The approach of Fr. Zafiris' article and that supported in Fr. John Meyendorff's book, *Marriage: An Orthodox Perspective,* as well as Fr. Demetrios Constantelos' book *Marriage, Sexuality and Celebacy: A Greek Orthodox Perspective* places the emphasis for the meaning of sex in general and contraception in particular on the whole experience of marriage as a holy, interpersonal relationship within the total framework of the Christian life. This approach sees marriage and the sex within it as having many purposes, none of which is seen as the crucial and exclusive purpose. When marriage and the sexual relations within it are approached from this sacramental perspective, then sexual relations between husband and wife are procreative in purpose, but also unitive.
>
> In this perspective the sexual relations of husband and wife have an intrinsic value: they unite husband and wife in flesh and soul in a bond of mutual love and commitment. The procreative purpose remains, however. But when children have been born, and the task is now the nurture of those children in a family environment of mutual love and in an atmosphere dominated by the relationship of the husband and wife, that sexual relationship is also significant for the whole tenor and well-being of the family life. Within this perspective contraception is not condemned, but rather it is seen as a means for the furthering of the goals and purposes of marriage as understood by the church. Normally, it would be wrong to use contraceptives to avoid the birth of any children. However, once children have been born, the use of contraceptives by the parents does not seem to violate any fundamental Christian understanding of marriage.[91]

Once again, the emphasis of the writers and the teachings of the Church is that sexual relations belong only within marriage as blessed by the Church (meaning that the couple has been married in the Orthodox Church through the sacrament of Holy Matrimony). Given this understanding, the term "safe sex" as preventing the spread of disease becomes unnecessary, since, if one is following the teachings of the Church a virgin couple marrying and being faithful to one another is inherently safe. Concern about becoming pregnant would follow the practice outlined above.

Pre-Marital Sexual Relations

It is not surprising that one out of every four teens are unsure if it is right or wrong to have sexual relations prior to marriage, given how much teens are inundated with sexual messages and images in their daily life, starting from the pre-teen years. The fact that only 5.57 percent of teens in the survey thought pre-marital sex was right is remarkable given the pervasive exploitation of young males and females in the media as sex objects and the constant portrayal of sex outside of marriage as normal and an everyday event without

---

[90] *Marriage: An Orthodox Perspective*, John Meyendorff, St. Vladimir's Seminary Press, p. 66.
[91] *Contemporary Moral Issues: Facing Orthodox Christians*, Stanley S. Harakas, Light & Life Publishing, Minneapolis, Minnesota, 1982, pages 80-81.

consequences. We need to better equip teens to make good choices concerning sexual relations and to be able to see through the multitude of sexual messages they receive on a daily basis. We want teens to see themselves as important, valuable and sacred, despite the messages they receive to the contrary, which tend to debase both males and females. Simply teaching teens that sexual intercourse is bad is insufficient and tends to leave teens further confused as to why they are having the physical and psychological feelings and urges that come along with puberty and thereafter. This approach typically leads teens to feel that they themselves are bad for having these feelings and for being attracted to people of the opposite sex.

One of our goals ought to be to develop within the hearts and minds of teens the understanding that virginity is something very good, something to strive for until marriage, and something not to be embarrassed about possessing, but in fact an accomplishment to be "proud" of keeping. We want them to remain virgin until marriage, not simply because they did what they were asked in not having sex, but that they valued themselves, the person they will marry, their relationship with God, and their sexual as created by God. Teens ought to see sexual relations as something very sacred and good and therefore an act not lightly undertaken. We want them to understand that the consequences of a sexual relation are something that they carry with themselves throughout their life. They do not forget it or the person they had sex with, as they give up to the other person a very special part of themselves in the bonding that takes place in a sexual relationship. The bond created in having sex with another person is very real and does not simply disappear once the relationship ends.

We should strive to help teens remain virgin (or stop having pre-marital sex) because we care about them now and care about their future marriage relationship. Sexual relations that occur outside of marriage are brought into the marriage in one form or another and can stand as an impediment to the marriage being successful. One who has had sex outside of the marriage and has experienced the breaking up of that relationship often finds it more difficult to be able to fully and freely give of himself or herself to the next "other person". When a relationship breaks off there is always hurt and pain in that separation, and this is especially true when sexual relations have been involved. All of us, teens and adults alike, build up walls to protect ourselves against past hurts. People who have broken off relationships tend to be more protective of their feelings and emotions with the next relationship. Having sex within a relationship is a life-changing event that greatly intensifies the depth of the relationship and therefore the intensity of the hurt at separation and therefore typically entails the building of higher and stronger walls to protect one when the next relationship comes along. We want our young people to be successful in marriage and to enjoy the full intensity of the marriage relationship and that includes being able to give themselves fully, freely and totally in their sexual relationship in the marriage. Being able to fully and freely give oneself to one's spouse through sexual relations is essential to the health and well-being of the marriage relationship.

The survey results strongly indicate an association between whether teens believe sex outside of marriage is right and whether they themselves engage in pre-marital sexual relations.[92] The obvious place to begin with preventing pre-marital sexual relations amongst

---

[92] Four percent of teens that believe that pre-marital sex is wrong have had a sexual relation, while 38 percent who believe pre-marital sex is right have had a sexual relationship.

teens is to begin with their attitude concerning sexuality and other related issues. We know from the survey that parents and clergy can have a profound impact on teen's attitudes concerning pre-marital sex.[93] It therefore makes sense that parents and clergy work together to discuss these issues with teens and dialogue with them about making good choices regarding their sexual purity.

Consideration should be given to providing opportunities where teens can safely spend time with their peers and learn to engage in healthy relationships with peers of the opposite sex without feeling pressured to have sex. These may be opportunities where both male and female teens can meet in well supervised events, free of alcohol and other drugs that tend to make pre-marital sex that much more likely to occur. [94] Likewise, efforts should be made to reduce, as much as possible, opportunities for males and females to be alone with one another, on such occasions as dating alone or no adults being home when teens are home from school and have a friend over. According to the survey, teens who did not have an adult present in the home when they arrived home from school were more than twice as likely to have had a sexual relationship than their peers who had an adult present when they arrived home from school.

Parents may want to give consideration towards discouraging their teens from dating during their early teen years, as statistically younger teens who dated were much more likely to have engaged in sexual behavior. The number of times a young teen had dated also raised the likelihood that they would be sexually active. For example, 20 percent of thirteen year olds who dated had intercourse, 8 percent of fourteen year olds, 7 percent of fifteen year olds, 12 percent of sixteen year olds, 21 percent of seventeen year olds and 29 percent of eighteen year olds. One can assume that not all eighteen year olds had sex only when they were eighteen, but may have had sex at an earlier age. Those teens that had not dated over the previous 12 months had no instances of pre-marital sex with the exception of seven teens, three of who reported being forced to have sex. In short adults can help teens remain virgin, by dialoging with them on what is appropriate, supporting them to remain virgins, consider placing more controls on dating, and to provide safe opportunities where teens can interact with their peers of the opposite sex, free from the pressures of feeling they are expected to have sex. The following material is offered to assist those dialoging with teens on the issue of sexuality.

The Church's view on Pre-marital sex

The Scriptures, writings of the Church Fathers and current theologians are all consistent in their view that sexual relations belong only within marriage. Sexual relations outside of marriage attempt to express a relationship and union which do not exist, a fact that eventually becomes evident in all such relationships. Sexual relations are seen as something good and necessary within marriage as an expression of a union (oneness) and commitment between husband and wife, neither of which exist outside of marriage. What is written in this section concerning pre-marital sex certainly also applies to sex outside of one's own

---

[93] See *Parental and Clergy effect on teen's views concerning pre-marital sex* in chapter 3.
[94] See *Effects of alcohol on sexual behavior* in chapter 3.

marriage and in fact extra-marital affairs add the consequence of breaking the marriage commitment and oneness of that marriage, a break which is often irreparable.

The Scriptures abound with prohibitions against pre-marital sexual relations, not because as some would say, "God does not want us to have fun," but because God loves us, understands us, and knows that such relationships can only bring harm, sadness and brokenness. In the book of Matthew, Jesus speaks concerning fornication (sexual relations outside of marriage):

> And he called the people to him and said to them, "Hear and understand: not what goes into the mouth defiles a man, but what comes out of the mouth, this defiles a man." Then the disciples came and said to him, "Do you know that the Pharisees were offended when they heard this saying?" He answered, "Every plant which my heavenly Father has not planted will be rooted up. Let them alone; they are blind guides. And if a blind man leads a blind man, both will fall into a pit." But Peter said to him, "Explain the parable to us." And he said, "Are you also still without understanding? Do you not see that whatever goes into the mouth passes into the stomach, and so passes on? But what comes out of the mouth proceeds from the heart, and this defiles a man. For out of the heart come evil thoughts, murder, adultery, fornication, theft, false witness, slander. These are what defile a man; but to eat with unwashed hands does not defile a man." (Matthew 15:10-20)

St. Paul writes in Galatians:

> For you were called to freedom, brethren; only do not use your freedom as an opportunity for the flesh, but through love be servants of one another. For the whole law is fulfilled in one word, "You shall love your neighbor as yourself." But if you bite and devour one another take heed that you are not consumed by one another.
>
> But I say, walk by the Spirit, and do not gratify the desires of the flesh. For the desires of the flesh are against the Spirit, and the desires of the Spirit are against the flesh; for these are opposed to each other, to prevent you from doing what you would. But if you are led by the Spirit you are not under the law. Now the works of the flesh are plain: fornication, impurity, licentiousness, idolatry, sorcery, enmity, strife, jealousy, anger, selfishness, dissension, party spirit, envy, drunkenness, carousing, and the like. I warn you, as I warned you before, that those who do such things shall not inherit the kingdom of God. But the fruit of the Spirit is love, joy, peace, patience, kindness, goodness, faithfulness, gentleness, self-control; against such there is no law. And those who belong to Christ Jesus have crucified the flesh with its passions and desires.
>
> If we live by the Spirit, let us also walk by the Spirit. Let us have no self-conceit, no provoking of one another, no envy of one another. (Galatians 5:13-25)

And in Ephesians Paul writes:

> Therefore be imitators of God, as beloved children. And walk in love, as Christ loved us and gave himself up for us, a fragrant offering and sacrifice to God.
>
> But fornication and all impurity or covetousness must not even be named among you, as is fitting among saints. Let there be no filthiness, nor silly talk, nor levity, which are not fitting; but instead let there be thanksgiving. Be sure of this, that no fornicator or impure man, or one who is covetous (that is, an idolater), has any inheritance in the kingdom of Christ and of God. Let no one deceive you with empty words, for it is because of these things that the wrath of God comes upon the sons of disobedience. Therefore do not associate with them, for once you were darkness, but now you are light in the Lord; walk as children of light (for the fruit of light is found in all that is good and right and true), and try to learn what is pleasing to the Lord. Take no part in the unfruitful works of darkness, but instead expose

them. For it is a shame even to speak of the things that they do in secret; but when anything is exposed by the light it becomes visible, for anything that becomes visible is light. (Ephesians 5:1-13)

The writings of the apostles also warn against fornication:

> My son, flee from all wickedness and from everything like it. Do not become angry, for anger leads to murder. Do not become jealous, or quarrelsome, or irritable, for from all these murders come. My child, do not give way to evil desire, for it leads to fornication. And do not use obscene language, or let your eye wander, for from all these come adulteries.[95]

The Shepherd of Hermes teaches that we should guard even our thoughts as these can lead to sin:

> Fourth Mandate
> I. PRESERVE CHASTITY
> 'I command you,' he said, 'to guard purity. Let it not enter your heart to think of another man's wife, nor about fornication, nor any such thing. If you do, you will commit a serious sin. Keep your wife in mind always and you will never fall into sin. For, if this desire comes into your heart, you will make a slip and you will commit sin, if any other such wicked thought enters you heart. For, a desire of this kind is a serious sin for the servant of God and, if anyone puts into execution such a wicked thought, he draws death upon himself. Be in your guard then: Keep this desire from you. Where holiness dwells, there, in the heart of a just man, lawlessness should not enter.'[96]

The Scriptural and Patristic teaching on sex outside of marriage whether it be physical sex, viewing pornography, "cyber sex" can be found consistently through the writings of other Church Fathers, such as John Chrysostom and Basil the Great. In this regard, Mathew records the words of Jesus, "But I say to you that everyone who looks at a woman with lust has already committed adultery with her in his heart." (Matthew 5:28) Current theologians similarly express these same views, as seen in the writings of John Meyendorff, Stanley Harakas, Alexander Schmemann, Thomas Hopko and others. Consistently the prohibitions against sex outside of marriage are because sex is sacred and blessed by God as a good and necessary ingredient to the health of marriage. The careless expression of sex before or outside the marriage bond cheapens and degrades both the intimacy of the sexual relation, its very beauty and ability to express oneness. Christ, the Scriptures and the Church Fathers consistently teach to guard one's words and thoughts as much as one's action, as one leads to the other. In sharing sexual intercourse, a person becomes one with the other person.[97] That intimate sharing does not just disappear when one moves onto the next relationship. When a person has sexual intercourse, they give fully of themselves to the other. Through intercourse they become one physically, emotionally and spiritually. If one has had sex before marriage they bring that experience and a "piece" of the other into their marriage. Sexual intercourse no longer becomes the unique bond of oneness shared only with husband and wife within the marriage but has had another complicating factor added and placed in-

---

[95] Didache or Teachings of the Apostles, Chapter 3:1-3, *FaithWorx*

[96] The Shepherd of Hermas, "Fourth Mandate: Preserve Chastity 1:1-3", FaithWorx CD

[97] Mark 10:8 and 1 Corinthians. 6:16

between the couple. With each sexual relationship and breaking of the relationships, one begins to put up more defenses and becomes more closed as a "thinking and feeling" person, placing more barriers between and within the marriage bond, therefore making true intimacy more difficult and strained. Young people should be urged to remain virgin until marriage, so as to allow for a deep and fulfilled marriage commitment and a more intimate sexual relationship with their spouse.

> For it has seemed good to the Holy Spirit and to us to lay upon you no greater burden than these necessary things: that you abstain from what has been sacrificed to idols and from blood and from what is strangled and from unchastity[98]. If you keep yourselves from these, you will do well. Farewell." (Acts 15:28-29 - instruction to the Gentiles)

> Shun immorality[99]. Every other sin which a man commits is outside the body; but the immoral man sins against his own body. Do you not know that your body is a temple of the Holy Spirit within you, which you have from God? You are not your own; you were bought with a price. So glorify God in your body. (1 Corinthians 6:18-19)

Homosexuality [100]

Another issue upon which teens exhibit a degree of confusion is that of homosexuality. Nearly one out of four teens was unsure whether homosexuality was right or wrong. When it came to equating homosexuality with the act of sex between people of the same sex the percentage of teens who saw homosexuality as right behavior dropped significantly. While 185 were not sure whether homosexuality was right or wrong, when they were asked if it was right or wrong for two people of the same sex to have a sexual relation only four of them said it was right and ninety-seven were unsure, while eighty-four stated it was wrong. A similar response was found from those who stated that homosexuality was right in question eighty-four of the survey. While fifty-one teens in question eighty-four said homosexual relations were right, only twenty-one of them said it was right for two people of the same sex to have a sexual relationship with one another (question 91). Further, of the fifty-one whom though homosexual relationships were right, only three of them have had a sexual relationship with someone of the same sex. Only three of the twenty-six teens that had sex with someone of the same sex as they thought homosexual relationships were right.

One might want to ask here how much of an influence has the current teachings on "tolerance and acceptance" of other lifestyles led to one out of every four teens being unsure whether homosexuality is right or wrong. Interestingly in this survey when teens were asked, "Is it right or wrong for someone else to have sex with a person of the same sex as them" the "not sure" dropped to 17 percent and when asked if it was right for them to do so, it dropped even further to 11 percent. In each case more teens respectively said it was wrong behavior. Young people in their everyday life are being confronted with the homosexual life style as normal and good, whether it is on television, the movies, at school, and in society in general. A decade ago homosexuality was a hidden lifestyle, today is much in the open and promoted as acceptable and even protected by law in many states. College students,

---

[98] Other translations use the word fornication
[99] Other translations use the word fornication
[100] What can be said of homosexuality also applies to Lesbian relationships

particularly females, state that on many college campuses it has become the fad to experiment with this lifestyle and behavior. Experimenting with homosexuality can be found on the high school and middle school level as well.

It is significant that just over one quarter of the teens in the survey had neither a parent or clergyman speak to them concerning homosexuality and that over one half had only one of these two people speak to them on this issue. This is significant when one looks at the data in the survey and realizes that a number of teens are not equating homosexuality with what the term means in terms of behavior. It evident from the survey, that honest and frank discussion on homosexuality needs to take place with teens. As a Church, we want our teens to be able to discern what is right and wrong for them and even for others, so that they can help their peers and eventually their own children make good decisions regarding their lifestyle choices. An important part of the discussion on homosexuality ought to be what is homosexuality and what does it mean in terms of our relationships with one another and with God. The following overview on homosexuality is presented as a starting point of this.

The Church's view on Homosexuality

Homosexuality is not new; writings as far back as the Old Testament deal with this issue. What is new in American Society is the current public display and promotion of this lifestyle and its protection by laws. Much of what was said before about sexual relations outside of marriage applies to homosexual relationships. In addition, the Scriptures and the Fathers of the Church speak out on this issue and classify this behavior as unnatural and immoral.[101] Adding to the complexity of this issue is the current claim that homosexuals may be genetically[102] predisposed to such behavior and therefore cannot help themselves but behave this way. Whether one accepts this argument or the argument that children become homosexual in reaction to unhealthy adult relationships is to demean such individuals by saying that they have no control over their passions or their personal direction in life. Whether heterosexual or homosexual we are all called to control our passions. Sex outside of marriage for a homosexual person is as wrong as it is for a heterosexual person. To claim one has more control over not sinning than the other is to deny personal freedom and the ability to fully choose one's actions. It is to say that the homosexual has less control over their urges than the heterosexual does and that one is freer than the other. The claim that they are naturally attracted to people of the same sex, so it is acceptable, is no more appropriate than the claim that a heterosexual person is attracted to people of the opposite sex and therefore should be free to express their sexual urges at anytime and with anyone they desire of the opposite sex. Likewise, the argument of genetic predisposition again demeans the person as saying they are incapable of choosing to do right. It is much like the argument of conducting genetic tests to see if someone is predisposed to be a thief or murder and therefore categorizing them and even limiting their activities just because they may posses such a gene, with no consideration for their own struggle to do right and refrain from

---

[101] Romans 1:26

[102] There is current evidence that there is no "homosexual gene", according to a study published in the, *Science*, during the week of April 25, 1999. George Rice and colleagues at the University of Western Ontario in London, Canada did the study. See "Gay Gene" in the Appendix.

acting on such predispositions. The Church calls us to be caring and loving to all people, but this does not mean that in loving all people we must accept all behavior as good. The Church has long taught that we are called to love all people but not all behaviors. When one condemns homosexual conduct, he or she condemns the conduct not the person. Despite the homosexual person's failings, we are still called to love them as a person, to treat them with respect, as we would expect to be treated in our own personal failing.

Harakas in his book *Contemporary Moral Issues* clearly outlines the Church's teaching on homosexual acts:

> Regarding homosexual acts, the traditional and exclusive teaching of the Church is condemnatory, seeing such acts as morally wrong. In the face of homosexual acts as well as all other expressions of wrongful sexual expression (fornication, adultery, prostitution, incest, bestiality, masturbation) the Church teaches that the only proper place for the exercise of the sexual function is in marriage. The evidence from the sources of the faith, without exception, considers homosexual acts as morally wrong. In the Old Testament, we read "If there is a man who lies with a male as those be with a woman, both of them have committed a detestable act. (Leviticus 20:13. Also, 18:22). Grave punishment was visited on the city of Sodom by God for this sin (Genesis 19:1-29) and as a result Sodomy is another name by which homosexual behavior is described. In speaking of this sinful act, the New Testament uses it to illustrate the "depraved passions" of fallen humanity: "their women exchanged the natural function for that which is unnatural, and in the same way the men abandoned the natural function of women and burned in their desire towards one another, men with men, committing indecent acts …" (Romans 1:24-28). Elsewhere, this evil is related with several others and severe punishment is promised:

> "Do you not know that the unrighteous will not inherit the kingdom of God? Do not be deceived; neither the immoral, nor idolaters, nor adulterers, nor homosexuals (arsenokoi-tai—literally, "men go to bed with men for sexual acts"), nor thieves, nor the greedy, nor drunkards, nor revilers, nor robbers will inherit the kingdom of God" (1 Corinthians 6:9-10. Also, 1 Timothy 1:8-10).

> The patristic tradition is no less unanimous and clear-cut in its judgment. From the 2nd century *Didache of the Twelve Apostles,* through the writings of the Fathers of the Golden Age of the Church such as St. Basil, St. John Chrysostom, St. Augustine, St. Gregory of Nyssa (4th and 5th centuries), through the sixth century Code of Justinian, the *Canons* of St. John the Faster (early 7th century) to the decisions of the 21st (1972), and 23rd (1976) Clergy-Laity statement on Homosexuality by the Standing Conference of Canonical Orthodox Bishops in the Americas, released in March of 1978, the teaching is consistent and unvarying: homosexual acts are immoral and wrong.[103]

Paul D. O'Callaghan writes in the Journal of Christian Bioethics,

> Consideration of the divine design and purpose of sex immediately reveals why homosex, adultery, fornication, prostitution, masturbation, and all other forms of sex outside of marriage are morally deviant. In none of these acts can the true realization of oneness in communion occur, because they are outside the God-established marital union, violations of it, or fundamentally disordered. All of these are true of homosexuality. Since the unitive drive for the experience of union is realized in the *conjuntio oppositorum*, the desire of man and woman to recreate their original oneness in Adam, it is clear that the desire for union

---

[103] Harakas, Contemporary Moral Issues, 93-94

with the same sex is a disordered passion. Something is very wrong when a male seeks to complete himself by union with another male. This is why the Apostle Paul argues that homosexuality is "against nature" (see Rom. 1:26-27). It is not just that the particular genital acts are ill fitted, unusual, and abhorrent. It is the fact that the very nature of the homosexual drive is at odds with how God created us as human beings, in His image, as male and female.[104]

Alcohol and Drug Abuse

According to the Teen Survey, more than four out of every ten teens say that they have been out drinking illegally with their friends in the past twelve months. Drinking instances began as early as age thirteen with 15 percent of teens in this age group stating they have been out drinking with their friends. At age fourteen the incident of drinking increased to 32 percent, age 15 to 39 percent, age sixteen to 55 percent, age seventeen to 62 percent and age eighteen to 79 percent. Overall, an equal percentage of females drank as males. For ages fourteen and sixteen significantly more[105] females drank than males and for ages thirteen and fifteen significantly more males drank than females, while for ages seventeen and eighteen more females drank than males though not significantly more.

As parents, youth workers, and concerned adults and as a Church we need to be concerned about the incidents of alcohol and other drug abuse. First of all drinking underage is illegal and can cause a teen to be arrested, suspended from school, kicked out of some colleges, and even prevent a teen from entrance to many colleges, if they have been arrested for drinking. Parents ought to be very concerned with this issue, because despite many years of nurturing their child for the best of colleges, a drinking related arrest can bar them from their "dream" college and perhaps college altogether, particularly if the drinking incident also gets the teen suspended or expelled from High School. The same can be said for other illegal drug use. A multitude of other risk factors come along with alcohol and other drug abuse; risk of death from the substance in question, driving deaths while under the influence—one of the leading killers of teens, brain damage, liver damage, and so forth. According to the teen survey alcohol also plays a major role in other risk taking behaviors such as pre-marital sex,[106] homosexuality[107], parental conflict[108] and the like. Teens who reported drinking alcohol are ten times more likely to have also tried or used other drugs compared to those who have not reported drinking. Those who drank alcohol were nearly three times more likely to also have smoked cigarettes than those who did not drink. Those who have tried or used other drugs were twelve times as likely to also have smoked compared to those who have not used other illegal drugs. Eighty percent of those who used cocaine reported being sexually active. When teens used both alcohol and other drugs the incidence of being sexually active rose to 54 percent compared to fewer than 4 percent for those who did not drink or use other illegal drugs. Similarly, those who smoked cigarettes were five times more likely to have engaged in pre-marital sex than their peers who did not smoke. It is also significant to note that of the ninety-three teens in the survey that have had

---

[104] Paul D. O'Callaghan, "Pseudosex in Pseudotheology", *Christian Bioethics: Non-Ecumenical Studies in Medical Morality*. April 1998, 93

[105] Refers to a greater percentage of females vs. the percentage of males within each gender.

[106] See *Effects of alcohol on sexual behavior* in chapter 3.

[107] See *Other significant parallels in one's behavior affecting other behaviors* in chapter 3.

[108] Teens who do not drink tend to get along better with their parents than those who do drink.

a sexual relationships 85 percent of them participate in one or more of the following behaviors; drank alcohol, smoked cigarettes, smoked marijuana, used cocaine, used other illegal drugs.

There is clear evidence that alcohol and other drug abuse clearly stands in the way of right behavior for our teens. These substances have a significant impact on the outcomes of teen behavior. We need to better educate our teens to these dangers. Just as important, we need to set the right example as parents, clergy, youth works and the Church as a whole, to appropriate behaviors concerning these substances. Most teens, as young as age 12, will tell you that it is very easy to obtain alcohol and other drugs, wherever and whenever they want them. We need to work towards building the self-esteem and confidence of our teens so that they understand they can have fun and live life very well and in fact better, without abusing alcohol and using other illegal drugs. We also want them to understand that their bodies are sacred and very important to them now and for the rest of their lives. We want them to care for their bodies both because it is essential to living a full life here and now and because it is the sacred temple of the Holy Spirit. The following section is offered as study material on this issue.

The Church's view on Alcohol and other Drug Abuse

> "Do you not know that your body is a temple of the Holy Spirit within you, which you have from God, and that you are not your own? For you were bought with a price; therefore glorify God in your body." (1Corinthians 6:19-20)

The Church's rational for being opposed to alcohol and drug abuse is found in St. Paul's letter to the Corinthians 6:19-20. In both cases, one who over indulges puts the body and mind at risk and in some cases harms and even destroys the body. It is a well-known fact that excessive alcohol consumption kills brain cells and affects the liver. Other drugs such as cigarettes, marijuana, cocaine, heroin and the like all affect the body and eventually harm and destroy various organs and can even lead to death. Aside from the physical harm caused by alcohol and other drugs, one's emotional and spiritual lives are directly affected. While certain forms of alcohol, such as wine, drunk in moderation, particularly with a meal, can in fact be healthy, overindulgence to the point that judgment becomes impaired can lead to loss of self-control and one's entering into sins one might not otherwise enter into. For example, in *The Orthodox Teen Survey* there was a direct link between alcohol consumption and those who were sexually active. Alcohol lowers ones ability to effectively control what is happening to oneself and impairs one's sense of judgment. The casual view, that alcohol consumption is normal amongst teens, has led many teens into situations that have caused them much harm. While a total prohibition of alcohol is not recommended since even the scriptures say that a little wine is good, the causal attitude in society about becoming intoxicated needs to be changed. Teens need to learn responsible alcohol consumption from the behavior of their parents and other adults in the community in addition to any other teaching on this matter.

Other drugs, from cigarettes to marijuana to heroin all fall into the category of having virtually no benefit and only provide harm to the body, mind and spirit, aside perhaps from some controlled medical uses. Such abuses of the body can be classified as a form of indirect suicide, in which the continued use of such substances over time will lead to the deterioration of the body and eventual death. If we take seriously the fact that our bodies are the temples of the Holy Spirit, then it becomes incumbent upon us to keep the body pure, healthy and sound. The Church puts the emphasis on the sacredness of the body and calls us to care for it, nurture it and protect it from all forms of defilement and harm. In caring for the body, keeping the body sound and pure, we also provide for our spiritual wellness and wholeness. The Church has always spoken of the person as a whole human being; emphasizing the sacredness of both body and soul. In the Resurrection accounts of Christ in the Scripture, it is emphasized that Jesus was raised both in Body and Spirit. By caring for one's body and keeping it pure, healthy and strong, a person also helps keep their spiritual life in order, as by disciplining the body one allows their spiritual life to guide them, rather than the cravings of the body.

Further Reading

Many issues were raised in *The Orthodox Teen Survey*, which were not covered in this chapter, due to the limitation of time and space. It is the hope of this author that others will further this work, by speaking, writing, teaching, and researching the issues raised in *The Orthodox Teen Survey*. It is the fervent desire and expectation of this author that the teens in this study, will themselves, desire a better life and will reach out to the Scriptures, writings of the Church Fathers, the liturgical services of the Church, to their pastors, youth workers, other clergy, their parents and adults in the Church community, in an effort to seek the truth and live life to its fullest. As a beginning to that process, the books listed below are suggested reading, both for teens and adults who are concerned with the issues highlighted in this project. It is further recommended that the reader take the time to read the sections of the appendix which supply additional information on the teachings of the Church on these matters; sections such as the *Sanctity of Life* messages and the *Synodal Affirmations on Marriage, Family, Sexuality, and the Sanctity of Life*.

An Orthodox View of Abortion, Rev. Fr. John Kowalczyk with forward by Fr. Anthony Coniaris. Gopher State Litho Co. Minneapolis, 1977.
Well written book on the Orthodox Church's position on Abortion.
Contemporary Moral Issues: Facing the Orthodox Christian, Stanley S. Harakas. Light and Life Publishing Company. Minneapolis, 1982.
This book is written for the lay reader, an easy to read book for understanding the Church's view on moral and ethical issues.
Living the Faith, Stanley S. Harakas. Light and Life Publishing Company. Minneapolis. 1992.
Written for clergy, youth workers and theologians, and those teaching moral and ethical issues
The Sacred Gift of Life, Fr John Breck. St Vladimir's Seminary Press, Crestwood, NY. 1999.
This book focuses on the unprecedented advances in bioethics over the past 30 years based on Scripture and Patristic tradition. It provides an overview of major theological themes that condition any Orthodox response to issues involving the creation and termination of human life.

CONCLUSION

Understanding where teens stand on various issues, as well as understanding their behavior, provides a starting point for moving young people into a deeper relationship with Jesus Christ and the Christian Community. The purpose of this survey is not to see how good or bad teens are today, but are motivated out of love for them and a desire that they seek *Life* and live it to its fullest. By understanding teen trends and behaviors, and using that condition as a starting point, one can better work with teens and assist them in their spiritual journey. For teens, bringing Christ, His teachings and way of life to bear upon their everyday life, starting with their personal struggles is the first step in this journey. However, it needs to be noted that simply sharing the Church's teaching on these issues, while very important and a necessary step, will never be sufficient alone to equip young people to deal with the multitude of struggles and obstacles they will confront in their life. There will always be new struggles and new situations not covered before. It needs to be understood that bringing young people into a relationship with Jesus Christ and His Church are essential to equipping young people to live life and successfully navigate this journey.

A person's relationship with Christ and His Church is created and developed through daily personal prayer, frequent readings of the Scripture and other writings of the Church, through consistent community worship in the Church, by frequent *prepared* participation in the Eucharist, and through strong healthy relationships with adults in the Christian Community. Christians are called to worship and glorify God in their heart, thoughts, and practice. Being human means having a strong understanding and practice of worshipping and giving thanks to God. It is out of this relationship with God that right living has meaning, direction and strength. It is through this relationship with Christ, that His words become alive in the listener as a guide to daily living. It is when a young person can hold the image of Christ's face in their heart and mind—looking into His eyes—that he or she can then measure all things in life as appropriate or inappropriate.

This means that a two-fold effort towards enabling young people to make right choices is needed. First there needs to be a conscious development of each teen's relationship with Christ, His Church, as well as the presence of healthy adult role models in the Christian Community. Secondly and simultaneously, dialogues need to take place on the issues confronting teens in their daily lives in a meaningful and open manner. Emphasis is placed on dialogue, to allow teens to work out their position on the issues in a way that allows them to confront their own thoughts and to ultimately come to terms with the Church's teaching. The goal here is to allow the teen to incorporate the Church's teaching into his or her own life in a way that will affect not only intellectual thoughts but also behavior. It should be noted that spiritual and physical growth comes through processes that take time and effort to internalize.

Earlier in this project, mention was made of the multitude of negative models teens have for living life. We need to provide as many positive adult and teen role models in the Christian Community as possible for our teens to emulate. As Christians we are all called to be saints, to be role models for one another, our children, and all who see us. The best way to promote healthy teen life is to promote healthy adult life, whether those adults be the clergy, parents, parish council members, church leaders, or other adults in the Christian Community with whom teens will come in causal or close contact. The *Orthodox Teen Study* demonstrated a clear connection between what teens thought and what they did. This study also showed a strong connection between adult involvement in teen lives and how teens thought on a variety of issues. Teens hear what adults say; even more they learn by how they see adults handle situations. Christian communities have a responsibility to live precisely as Christian communities, because others are dependent upon that example for their salvation. The Church community is encouraged to be open to the young people in their communities and to be aware of their Christian responsibility to nurture young people as outlined in the first chapter of this book.

In closing, it is recommended that adults spend more time with young people. While quality time is important; unless adults are around long enough (quantity) teens will never feel adults have the time or concern to listen to them and their concerns. Parents, clergy and other committed Christians who are concerned about the well being of teens in their community are encouraged to spend open time with teens, to dialogue with them on the issues that concern them and assist them in developing a healthy understanding of life and themselves. One of the major factors in keeping teens active in the Christian Community is whether they feel welcomed, listened to, and feels as though they have a purpose for being there. Communities are encouraged to actively engage teens in the life of the community in meaningful and fulfilling roles, as well as to engage them in healthy relationships with members of the Christian Community.

It is the hope of this author that the reader will utilize this project towards better understanding teens, as a means of engaging teens in healthy discussions on the issues raised here. It is also the hope that teens will engage one another in meaningful discussion on these issues and that they will encourage one another to make right choices. Most importantly, teens are urged to continue to love and uplift one another in the Lord.

> A new commandment I give to you, that you love one another; even as I have loved you, that you also love one another. By this all men will know that you are my disciples, if you have love for one another." (John13:34-35)

APPENDIX

Mission Statement for Youth Ministry

Living the Orthodox Faith in Christ
Through Worship, Witness, Service and Fellowship

Statement of Purpose

We believe that the Goal of Orthodox Christian Youth Ministry is the integration of each young person fully into the total life of the Church. We believe that Orthodox Christians must commit themselves to living the Orthodox Faith daily. Worship, Witness, Service and Fellowship are the natural expressions of that commitment. We define them as follows:

WORSHIP - For Orthodox Christians, corporate worship is the sacramental expression of and participation in Holy Tradition, and is the indispensable foundation of youth ministry at all levels. Upon this foundation, we must cultivate a daily personal prayer life and reading of Holy Scripture.

WITNESS - Christ calls us to be His witness in the world. We must enable our youth to express their faith for themselves and to others in order to be true witnesses to Christ and the Orthodox Faith.

SERVICE - Christ came not to be served, but to serve. We need to move our youth to do the same. We honor and glorify God by loving and serving mankind in the name of Jesus Christ, using our God-given gifts and talents.

FELLOWSHIP - The Holy Trinity is the perfect model of fellowship; the Father, Son, and Holy Spirit share perfect communion and exist in perfect love as a community. By gathering together in fellowship, and by showing love for one another in Christ, we emulate the life of the Holy Trinity in our daily life.

Our ultimate goal must be to see that our youth grow to love Christ and His Church and to pursue a righteous way of life.

Our movement integrates the Camping Programs, Teen SOYO, Campus Ministry and the Fellowship of St. John the Divine - programs designed to meet the needs of varying age groups. We will attain these goals by training youth ministers, both clergy and lay, to serve at all levels, and by developing and providing relevant resource materials.

Antiochian Archdiocese Youth Ministry: http://www.antiochian.org/youth

Antiochian Archdiocese Home Page: http://www.antiochian.org

Orthodox Christian Teen Survey
Orthodox Christian Teen Survey

General Information

1. I am:
   F. Female **M.** Male
2. My grade in school is:
   7 8 9 10 11 12 13 (College Freshman)
   14 (College Sophomore)
3. I go to the following type of School:
   A. Public B. Private C. Parochial D. Home
4. My age is:
   12 13 14 15 16 17 18 19
5. My Orthodox Parish is in the following Region:
   **Can-Am - Eastern - New England -
   Midwest - Southeast -Southwest - Western**
6. I live in the following Country:
   United States - Canada

Your Family

7. How many children are there in your family?
   1 2 3 4 5 6 7 8 9
8. My family is helpful to me with my schoolwork.
   Y. Yes N. No
9. My family talks openly about issues that concern me.
   Y. Yes N. No
10. Is your mother an Orthodox Christian?
    Y. Yes N. No
10a. If not Orthodox what is she? _____
11. Is your Father an Orthodox Christian?
    Y. Yes N. No
11a. If not Orthodox what is he? _____
12. Does your family observe the Fast before Christmas?
    Y. Yes N. No
13. Does your family observe the Fast for Great Lent?
    Y. Yes N. No

My parents have discussed with me their feeling concerning:

14. Pre-marital sexual relations.
    Y. Yes N. No
15. Birth Control
    Y. Yes N. No
16. Abortion
    Y. Yes N. No
17. Euthanasia (or mercy killing)
    Y. Yes N. No
18. Homosexuality
    Y. Yes N. No
19. Aids and other sexually transmitted diseases
    Y. Yes N. No
20. Stealing
    Y. Yes N. No
21. Lying
    Y. Yes N. No
22. Truthfulness
    Y. Yes N. No
23. School grades
    Y. Yes N. No
24. Their expectations for my career
    Y. Yes N. No
25. Their expectations for my life
    Y. Yes N. No
26. Marriage
    Y. Yes N. No
27. Fidelity (or faithfulness) in Marriage
    Y. Yes N. No
28. Dating
    Y. Yes N. No
29. Their Religious Faith
    Y. Yes N. No

My family discusses:

30. Issues concerning our community
    Y. Yes N. No
31. Issues concerning our Church
    Y. Yes N. No
32. Issues concerning the World
    Y. Yes N. No
33. Issues concerning me
    Y. Yes N. No
34. Issues concerning other family members
    Y. Yes N. No
35. My school day
    Y. Yes N. No
36. Family problems and interests
    Y. Yes N. No
37. News and current events
    Y. Yes N. No
38. School
    Y. Yes N. No
39. Before eating Dinner someone in my family says a prayer
    Y. Yes N. No

My Parents

40. Do you think your parents are:
    A. Too strict with you B. not strict enough
    C. just about right
41. How well would you say you get along with your parents:
    A. Very well B. fairly well C. not very well?

42. Would you say you get along better with your mother or your father?
    A. Mother B. Father   C. Both   D. Neither
43. My parent's involvement in my life is....
    A. Just right B. Not enough C. Too much
44. Are your birth parents: (If adopted answer for your adopted parents)
    A. Married to each other.   B. Never married.
    C. Separated D. Divorced E. Mother deceased F. Father deceased
45. If you answered anything above other than "married to each other", are one or both of your birth parents remarried to someone else?
    Y. Yes N. No
46. When you arrive home from school is there an adult home when you get home?
    Y. Yes N. No

What You Think and Do
47. On average, how much time do you spend each day on a computer?
    A. None B. less than 1 hour C. 1-2 hours D. 3-4 hours E. more than 4 hours

48. On average, how much time do you spend each day on the Internet?
    A. None B. less than 1 hour C. 1-2 hours D. 3-4 hours E. more than 4 hours

49. On average, how much time do you spend in an on-line chat room?
    A. None B. less than 1 hour C. 1-2 hours D. 3-4 hours E. more than 4 hours

50. In general, are you satisfied or dissatisfied with the way things are going in your own personal life?
    A. Very satisfied   B. Somewhat satisfied C. dissatisfied

---

Choose one of the answers for the following questions:
N. Never
O. Once
T. Two to six times
M. More than six times

51. I smoked cigarettes in the last month

52. I smoked cigars in the last month

53. I chewed tobacco in the last month

54. I have smoked marijuana in my lifetime.
55. I have used cocaine in my lifetime.

56. I have tried other illegal drugs, besides marijuana or cocaine in my lifetime.

57. I have smoked cigarettes or cigars in my lifetime.

58. I have chewed tobacco in my lifetime.

59. In the past twelve months I have drunk alcohol with my friends.

60. In the past twelve months I have drunk alcohol by myself.

How much does each of the following influence how you think and act?
Your choices are:
V. Very Much S. Somewhat N. Very little or not at all

61. Books
62. Friends
63. Church Youth Group
64. Parents
65. Magazines
66. Movies
67. Music
68. Religion
69. School
70. Television
71. The Internet
72. Computers
73. Church School Teachers
74. Pastor
75. Church Youth Workers (Teen Advisors)
76. School Teachers
77. Guidance Counselor

---

78. In the following list, number from 1-3 the **three greatest** problems you face.
    Select *three*
    A. Being Liked
    B. School Grades
    C. Career uncertainties
    D. Growing Pains
    E. Fears
    F. Getting along with parents
    G. Financing college
    H. School problems
    I. Drug abuse
    J. Fear of war
    K. Peer pressures
    L. Weight problems
    M. Concern about AIDS

N. Concern about Sexually Transmitted Disease other than AIDS
O. Economic problems
P. Alcohol abuse
Q. Depression *(Continues onto the next page)*
R. Teen pregnancy
S. Pressure to have sex
T. Homosexuality
U. Birth Control
V. Abortion
W. Violence
X. Other _____

79. What are the **three greatest** problems your best friend faces? Number 1-3.
Select three
A. Being Liked
B. School Grades
C. Career uncertainties
D. Growing Pains
E. Fears
F. Getting along with parents
G. Financing college
H. School problems
I. Drug abuse
J. Fear of war
K. Peer pressures
L. Weight problems
M. Concern about AIDS
N. Concern about Sexually Transmitted Disease other than AIDS
O. Economic problems
P. Alcohol abuse
Q. Depression
R. Teen pregnancy
S. Pressure to have sex
T. Homosexuality
U. Birth Control
V. Abortion
W. Violence
X. Other _____

80. What do you feel are the **three greatest** problems facing people your age? Number 1-3.
Select three
A. Being Liked
B. School Grades
C. Career uncertainties
D. Growing Pains
E. Fears
F. Getting along with parents
G. Financing college
H. School problems
I. Drug abuse
J. Fear of war

K. Peer pressures
L. Weight problems
M. Concern about AIDS
N. Concern about Sexually Transmitted Disease other than AIDS
O. Economic problems
P. Alcohol abuse
Q. Depression
R. Teen pregnancy
S. Pressure to have sex
T. Homosexuality
U. Birth Control
V. Abortion
W. Violence
X. Other _____.

Right and Wrong.
In your opinion, is each of the actions in the following questions morally right or wrong? These are the possible responses:
R. Morally right.   N. Not Sure.   W. Morally Wrong

81. Having an abortion for reasons other than saving the physical life of the mother.
82. Having an abortion to save the physical life of the mother.
83. Having an abortion for any reason.
84. Homosexual relationships.
85. Sexual Intercourse between two unmarried 16 year-olds who love each other.
86. Cheating on a test at school.
87. Lying to one's parents.
88. Sixteen-year-olds drinking a couple of beers at a party.
89. Stealing clothes from a store that I know makes a lot of money.
90. For you to have sex with someone of the same sex as you.
91. For someone else to have sex with a person of the same sex as them.
92. Capital Punishment (Putting someone to death for a crime they have committed)
93. Euthanasia (Helping someone who is ill end their life to free them from suffering or because they are elderly and feel they have no more to offer)
94. Have sexual intercourse before you are married.
95. When you are married to have a sexual relationship with someone other than the person you are married to.
96. Use birth control before you are married.
97. To look at pornographic material.
98. To have "cyber sex" with someone in a computer chat rooms on the Internet.

99. To help those who are less fortunate than you.
100. To help someone stand up against injustice, when you will not gain anything from doing so.

Relationships

101. How many times in the past twelve months have you been out on a date (such as going to a party or movie with one person of the opposite sex)?
    A. None
    B. One or two times
    C. Three to five times
    D. Six to nine times
    E. Ten to nineteen times
    F. Twenty times or more

102. Is it difficult for you to talk to other teens of the opposite sex?
    Y. Yes
    N. No

103. How often do you think about sex?
    A. Very often
    B. Sometimes
    C. Never

104. Have you ever had sexual intercourse ("gone all the way" or "made love")?
    A. Never
    B. Yes, one time
    C. Yes, two to five times
    D. Yes, six times or more
    E. I don't know what sexual intercourse is.

105. Have you ever had sexual relations with someone of the same sex as you?
    A. Never
    B. Yes, one time
    C. Yes, two to five times
    D. Yes, six times or more
    E. I don't know what sexual relations are.

106. Have you ever been forced to have a sexual relation you did not want?
    Y. Yes
    N. No

107. Have you ever been sexually harassed?
    Y. Yes
    N. No

108. Teen Pregnancy - If you are a female, have you ever been pregnant, or if you are a male have you ever gotten someone pregnant?
    Y. Yes
    N. No

109. Do you have a teenage friend who has ever been pregnant and was not married at the time?
    Y. Yes
    N. No

110. Have you ever-considered committing suicide (killing yourself)?
    Y. Yes
    N. No

111. Have you ever had an eating disorder?
    Y. Yes
    N. No

What I worry About

How much do you worry about the following statements? Your Choices are:
V. Very much
S. Somewhat
N. Not at all or Very little

112. The violence around me.
113. Being discriminated against.
114. That I may take illegal drugs.
115. That I will be pressured into having sex before I am ready or against my will.
116. That I may have an eating disorder.
117. That I might commit suicide (kill myself).
118. That my parents will physically hurt me.
119. That I might die soon.
120. That I might not get into a good college.
121. That my parents will get divorced.

My Christian Life

122. Are you an Orthodox Christian?
    Y. Yes
    N. No

123. How would you rate your Church Attendance:
    M. more than once a week
    W. weekly
    A. a few times a month
    O. once a month
    L. less than once a month but more than six times a year
    S. less than six times a year but I still go more than once a year

Y. once a year

I. I do not go to Church

124. Do you feel close to your Church Community?
Y. Yes
N. No

125. Which of the following statements comes closest to your view of God?
K. I know for sure that God exists.
M. I am mostly sure that God exists.
N. I'm not sure if God exists.
D. I don't think there is a God
S. I am sure there is no such thing as God.

126. Which of the following statements is closest to your view of Jesus?
T.   Jesus is the Son of God who became a man to save us. He died on the cross for our salvation and rose from the dead.
W.   Jesus was a man anointed by God at his baptism to be God's Son and he died on the cross for our salvation and rose from the dead.
J.   Jesus was the Son of God but I doubt he rose from the dead.
A.   Jesus was a great man who lived long ago, but I do not think he was really the Son of God.
G.   Jesus was a great prophet, but not really the Son of God.
N.   I am not sure that Jesus existed

127. Do you believe there is a heaven where people who love God and have died are with God?
Y. Yes
NS. I am not sure Heaven exists
N. No

128. Do you believe there is a hell where those who hate God and have died are in eternal punishment?
Y. Yes
NS. I am not sure Hell exists
N. No

129. My religious beliefs greatly influence how I act at school and with my friends.
M. Most of the time
S. Some of the time
R. Rarely or never

Do you feel that the Church responds in a meaningful way to today's problems such as:

130. Problems about drugs and alcohol?
Y. Yes
N. No

131. Sexual Issues such as abortion and Aids?
Y. Yes
N. No

132. Problems of marriage and divorce?
Y. Yes
N. No

133. Morality in government?
Y. Yes
N. No

134. World problems, war and poverty?
Y. Yes
N. No

If you had a serious moral matter to discuss would you discuss it with your:

135. Your Pastor?
Y. Yes
N. No

136. Another Priest besides your pastor?
Y. Yes
N. No

137. Another adult in your parish?
Y. Yes
N. No

138. A Church schoolteacher?
Y. Yes
N. No

139. Your Youth Group Advisor or Director?
Y. Yes
N. No

140. A teacher at school?
Y. Yes
N. No

141. A Friend?
Y. Yes
N. No

142. Your friend's parent?
Y. Yes
N. No

143. An aunt or uncle?
Y. Yes
N. No

144. No one?
Y. Yes
N. No

145. How important are your religious beliefs to you?
A. Very important   B. Fairly important

C. Not too important   D. Not at all important

What moral and or ethical issues listed below has a clergyman from your Church discussed with you individually, as a member of your youth group, or from the pulpit:

146. Capital Punishment
   Y. Yes
   N. No
147. Cloning
   Y. Yes
   N. No
148. Abortion
   Y. Yes
   N. No
149. Pre-marital sex
   Y. Yes
   N. No
150. Birth control
   Y. Yes
   N. No
151. Adultery
   Y. Yes
   N. No
152. Euthanasia
   Y. Yes
   N. No
153. Homosexuality
   Y. Yes
   N. No

---

154. Have you ever attended Antiochian Village Camp in Pennsylvania?
   Y. Yes
   N. No

   If you answered "No" please skip to question 158.
   If you attended Antiochian Village Camp please answer the next three questions:
155. Did you enjoy Camp?
   Y. Yes
   N. No
156. Did you learn more about your Orthodox Faith while at Antiochian Village Camp?
   Y. Yes
   N. No
157. Would you go back to Antiochian Village Camp, if you had the opportunity?
   Y. Yes
   N. No

---

158. Have you ever attended Camp St. Nicholas in Frazier Park, California?
   Y. Yes
   N. No

   If you answered "No" please skip to question 162

   If you attended Camp St. Nicholas, please answer the next three questions:
159. Did you enjoy Camp?
   Y. Yes
   N. No
160. Did you learn more about your Orthodox Faith while at Camp St. Nicholas?
   Y. Yes
   N. No
161. Would you go back to Camp St. Nicholas, if you had the opportunity?
   Y. Yes
   N. No

---

162. Have you attended an Orthodox Camp, other than the ones mentioned above in questions 154 and 158?
   Y. Yes
   N. No

   If you answered "No" please go to question 166.

   If you attended Camp other than Antiochian Village or Camp St. Nicholas, please answer the next three questions:
163. Did you enjoy Camp?
   Y. Yes
   N. No
164. Did you learn more about your Orthodox Faith while at this Camp?
   Y. Yes
   N. No

165. Would you go back to this camp, if you had the opportunity?
   Y. Yes
   N. No

---

166. Have you ever attended your Regional Parish Life Conference?
   Y. Yes
   N. No
   If you answered "No" please skip to question 172.

If you attended your Regional Parish Life Conference please answer the following five questions:

167. Did you enjoy the Regional Parish Life Conference?
Y. Yes
N. No

168. Did you learn anything new about your Orthodox Faith at this conference?
Y. Yes
N. No

169. Did you meet new Friends at this conference?
Y. Yes
N. No

170. Did you feel welcomed?
Y. Yes
N. No

171. If you have the opportunity, will you attend another Regional Parish Life Conference?
Y. Yes
N. No

_____

172. Are you a member of Teen SOYO or another Youth Group in your parish other than Church School?
Y. Yes
N. No

173. How comfortable do you feel in sharing your Orthodox Faith with others?
A. Very comfortable
B. Somewhat comfortable
C. Not comfortable
D. I will not share it.

174. Would you recommend your church to a friend who does not belong to another Church?
Y. Yes
N. No
NS. Not sure

175. Do you feel that you have a relationship with God?
Y. Yes
N. No

176. Are you a convert to the Orthodox Church?
Y. Yes
N. No

177. Do you feel comfortable in the Orthodox Church you now attend?
Y. Yes
N. No

178. Do you feel comfortable attending Regional Conferences and Retreats?
Y. Yes

N. No
NA. Never attended one

179. Do you feel that the Ten Commandments are relevant to your life?
Y. Yes
N. No

180. Have others asked you to join a Church or Religious group, other than the Orthodox Church?
Y. Yes
N. No

If you said yes, which one (s)?
180a. _____

181. Has anyone ever asked you to join a cult?
Y. Yes
N. No

If you said yes, which one(s)?
181a. _____

182. Do you ever discuss your religion with your friends?
Y. Yes
N. No

183. Do your friends ever seriously challenge what you believe in?
Y. Yes
N. No

184. Do your friends ever challenge your belief in Jesus Christ?
Y. Yes
N. No

185. Do you feel prepared to discuss your Orthodox Faith with your friends?
Y. Yes
N. No

Rate how well you feel your church does in each of the areas listed below.
Your choices are:
E. Excellent
G. Good
O. Okay
F. Fair
P. Poor

186. Help you learn about the Bible
187. Help you learn what it means to be an Orthodox Christian?
188. Help in meeting your spiritual needs?
189. Help you in understanding today's problems?

190. Help you learn what is special about you?
191. Help your religious faith grow?
192. Help you make friends?
193. Help you to get to know adults who care about you?
194. Help you to help other people?
195. Help you learn about what is right or wrong?
196. Help you learn about sex and sexual values?

197. Help you learn about alcohol and other drugs, and what your values about them should be?
198. Provide lots of fun and good times?
199. Help you learn what a Christian should do about big issues such as poverty, war, and loneliness.
200. Show compassion and love to you.
201. Allow you as a teen to have a role in the ministry of the Church.

_____

202. How often do you pray alone:
    F. Frequently O. Occasionally
    H. Hardly ever N. Never

203. Describe how often you normally attend Church Services:
    M. More than once a week W. Once a week
    A. a few times a month O. Once a month
    L. Less than once a month I. I do not attend Church

204. How often do you read the Bible?
    D. Daily W. Weekly M. Monthly
    L. Less than Monthly N. Never

205. In the Past 30 days have you watched any religious programs on television?
    Y. Yes
    N. No

206. In the Past 30 days have you listened to any religious programs on radio?
    Y. Yes
    N. No

Who would you go to...

If you were in the following situations, to whom would you most likely turn to for help or advice? For each situation, choose one of these answers:
P. Parent or guardian
F. A friend my own age
A. An adult friend or relative
PR. A priest
Y. A parish youth worker or advisor
S. School counselor
O. On-line computer chat room
N. Nobody

207. If I were having trouble in school, I would turn to _____.

208. If I were wondering how to handle my feelings, I would turn to _____.

209. If some of my friends started using alcohol or other drugs, I would turn to _____.

210. If I had a question about sex, I would turn to _____.

211. If I were feeling guilty about something I had done, I would turn to _____.

212. If I were deciding what to do with my life, I would turn to _____.

213. If I were deciding whether it was right or wrong to have an abortion I would turn to _____.

214. If I were struggling with a moral or ethical issue I would turn to _____.

Orthodox Christian
Teen Survey Results

Questions: **Total Respondents: 790**

1. My sex is:	F	446	56.46%
	M	344	43.54%
2. My grade in school is:	6	1	0.13%
	7	40	5.06%
	8	127	16.08%
	9	165	20.89%
	10	140	17.72%
	11	132	16.71%
	12	121	15.32%
	13	48	6.08%
	14	12	1.52%
	15	4	0.51%
3. I go to the following type of School:	Home	23	2.91%
	Parochial	36	4.56%
	Private	127	16.08%
	Public	603	76.33%
4. My age is:	12	25	3.16%
	13	145	18.35%
	14	143	18.10%
	15	145	18.35%
	16	135	17.09%
	17	35	17.09%
	18	38	4.81%
	19	21	2.66%
	20	3	0.38%
5. My Orthodox Parish is in the following Region:	Can-Am	69	8.73%
	Eastern	144	18.23%
	Midwest	158	20.00%
	New England	62	7.85%
	Southeast	77	7.85%
	Southwest	110	13.92%
	Western	170	21.52%
6. I live in the following Country:	CA	42	5.32%
	US	748	94.68%
7. How many children are there in your family?	1	40	5.06%
	2	230	29.11%
	3	286	36.20%
	4	140	17.72%
	5	57	7.22%
	6	19	2.41%
	7	13	1.65%
	8	2	0.25%
	9	3	0.38%
8. My family is helpful to me with my schoolwork.	No	116	14.68%
	Sometimes	4	0.51%
	Yes	668	84.56%
9. My family talks openly about issues that concern	No	155	19.62%
	Sometimes	2	0.25%
	Yes	627	79.37%
10. Is your Mother an Orthodox Christian? If not, what is she?	Orthodox	733	92.78%
	Roman Catholic	33	4.18%

	No Faith	10	1.27%
	Lutheran	3	0.38%
	Presbyterian	2	0.25%
	Maronite	2	0.25%
	Episcopal	2	0.25%
	Protestant	1	0.13%
	Muslim	1	0.13%
	Eastern Catholic	1	0.13%
	Baptist	1	0.13%
	Agnostic	1	0.13%
11. Is your Father an Orthodox Christian? If not, what is he?	Orthodox	696	88.10%
	Roman Catholic	37	4.68%
	No Faith	27	3.42%
	Do Not Know	7	0.89%
	Protestant	4	0.51%
	Atheist	3	0.38%
	Methodist	3	0.38%
	Lutheran	2	0.25%
	Baptist	2	0.25%
	Jewish	2	0.25%
	Agnostic	1	0.13%
	Episcopal	1	0.13%
	Calvinist	1	0.13%
	Muslim	1	0.13%
	Pentecostal	1	0.13%
	Armenian	1	0.13%
	Jehovah Witness	1	0.13%
12. Does your family observe the Fast before Christmas?	No	348	44.05%
	Sometimes	2	0.25%
	Yes	427	54.05%
13. Does your family observe the Fast for Great Lent?	No	92	11.65%
	Sometimes	5	0.63%
	Yes	689	87.22%
14. My parents have discussed with me their feelings about—Pre-marital sexual relations.	No	247	31.27%
	Yes	543	68.73%
15. My parents have discussed with me their feelings about—Birth Control	No	492	62.28%
	Yes	297	37.59%
16. My parents have discussed with me their feelings about—Abortion	No	323	40.89%
	Yes	464	58.73%
17. My parents have discussed with me their feelings about—Euthanasia (or mercy killing)	No	514	65.06%
	Yes	273	34.56%
18. My parents have discussed with me their feelings about—Homosexuality	No	291	36.84%
	Sometimes	1	0.13%
	Yes	498	63.04%
19. My parents have discussed with me their feelings about—AIDS and other sexually transmitted diseases	No	278	35.19%
	Yes	511	64.68%
20. My parents have discussed with me their feelings about—Stealing	No	118	14.94%
	Yes	672	85.06%
21. My parents have discussed with me their feelings about—Lying	No	46	5.82%
	Sometimes	1	0.13%
	Yes	741	93.80%
22. My parents have discussed with me their feelings about—Truthfulness	No	29	3.67%
	Yes	760	96.20%
23. My parents have discussed with me their feelings about—School grades	No	11	1.39%
	Yes	775	98.10%
24. My parents have discussed with me their feelings about—Their expectations for my career	No	190	24.05%
	Yes	598	75.70%
25. My parents have discussed with me their feelings about—Their expectations for my life	No	187	23.67%
	Yes	601	76.08%
26. My parents have discussed with me their feelings	No	224	28.35%

about — Marriage	Yes	564	71.39%
27. My parents have discussed with me their feelings about—Fidelity (or faithfulness) in marriage	No	279	35.32%
	Yes	508	64.30%
28. My parents have discussed with me their feelings about—Dating	No	149	18.86%
	Yes	638	80.76%
29. My parents have discussed with me their feelings about—Their Religious Faith	No	106	13.42%
	Yes	680	86.08%
30. My family discusses—Issues concerning our community	No	242	30.63%
	Sometimes	3	0.38%
	Yes	542	68.61%
31. My family discusses … Issues concerning our Church	No	88	11.14%
	Sometimes	3	0.38%
	Yes	698	88.35%
32. My family discusses … Issues concerning the World	No	149	18.86%
	Sometimes	3	0.38%
	Yes	638	80.76%
33. My family discusses … Issues concerning me	No	49	6.20%
	Sometimes	1	0.13%
	Yes	739	93.54%
34. My family discusses … Issues concerning other family members	No	67	8.48%
	Sometimes	1	0.13%
	Yes	721	91.27%
35. My family discusses … My school day	No	142	17.97%
	Sometimes	3	0.38%
	Yes	644	81.52%
36. My family discusses … Family problems and interests	No	84	10.63%
	Sometimes	0	0%
	Yes	705	89.24%
37. My family discusses … News and current events	No	154	19.49%
	Sometimes	2	0.25%
	Yes	631	79.87%
38. My family discusses … School	No	34	4.30%
	Sometimes	0	0%
	Yes	756	95.70%
39. Before eating Dinner someone in my family says a prayer	No	336	42.53%
	Sometimes	7	0.89%
	Yes	447	56.58%
40. Do you think your parents are:	Just about right	563	71.27%
	Not strict enough	16	2.03%
	Too strict	211	26.71%
41. How well would you say you get along with your parents:	Fairly Well	374	47.34%
	Not Very Well	47	5.95%
	Very Well	367	46.46%
42. Would you say you get along better with your	Both	327	41.39%
	Father	166	21.01%
	Mother	267	33.80%
	Neither	30	3.80%
43. My parent's involvement in my life is….	Just right	580	73.42%
	Not enough	54	6.84%
	Too much	154	19.49%
44. Are your birth parents: (If adopted, answer for your adopted parents)	Divorced	69	8.73%
	Father Deceased	14	1.77%
	Married to each other	688	87.09%
	Mother Deceased	1	0.13%
	Never married	5	0.63%
	Separated	7	0.89%
45. If you answered anything above other than "married to each other." are one or both of your birth parents remarried to	No	50	6.33%
	Not applicable	1	0.13%

someone else?	Yes	48	6.08%
46. When you arrive home from school, is there an adult there?	No	260	32.91%
	Sometimes	25	3.16%
	Yes	481	60.89%
47. On average, how much time do you spend each day on a computer?	1-2 hours	283	35.82%
	3-4 hours	69	8.73%
	Less than 1 hour	272	34.43%
	More than 4 hours	27	3.42%
	None	136	17.22%
48. On average, how much time do you spend each day on the Internet?	1-2 hours	176	22.28%
	3-4 hours	28	3.54%
	Less than 1 hour	265	33.54%
	More than 4 hours	20	2.53%
	None	298	37.72%
49. On average, how much time do you spend in an on-line chat room?	1-2 hours	61	7.72%
	3-4 hours	14	1.77%
	Less than 1 hour	194	24.56%
	More than 4 hours	9	1.14%
	None	510	64.56%
50. In general, are you satisfied or dissatisfied with the way things are going in your own personal	Dissatisfied	63	7.97%
	Somewhat Satisfied	458	57.97%
	Very Satisfied	266	33.67%
51. I smoked cigarettes in the last month	1-2 Times	47	5.95%
	2-6 Times	46	5.82%
	more than 6 times	46	5.82%
	Never	627	79.37%
	Yes	22	2.78%
52. I smoked cigars in the last month	1-2 Times	51	6.46%
	2-6 Times	28	3.54%
	more than 6 times	5	0.63%
	Never	695	87.97%
	Yes	9	1.14%
53. I chewed tobacco in the last month	1-2 Times	8	1.01%
	2-6 Times	3	0.38%
	more than 6 times	7	0.89%
	Never	766	96.96%
	Yes	2	0.25%
54. I have smoked marijuana in my lifetime	1-2 Times	55	6.96%
	2-6 Times	34	4.30%
	more than 6 times	48	6.08%
	Never	648	82.03%
55. I have used cocaine in my lifetime	1-2 Times	3	0.38%
	2-6 Times	7	0.89%
	more than 6 times	5	0.63%
	Never	768	97.22%
56. I have tried other illegal drugs, besides marijuana or cocaine in my lifetime	1-2 Times	18	2.28%
	2-6 Times	11	1.39%
	more than 6 times	12	1.52%
	Never	745	94.30%
57. I have smoked cigarettes or cigars in my lifetime	1-2 Times	112	14.18%
	2-6 Times	109	13.80%
	more than 6 times	154	19.49%
	Never	410	51.90%
58. I have chewed tobacco in my lifetime	1-2 Times	33	4.18%
	2-6 Times	14	1.77%
	more than 6 times	16	2.03%
	Never	723	91.52%
59. In the past twelve months I have drunk alcohol with m friends	1-2 Times	103	13.04%
	2-6 Times	135	17.09%
	more than 6 times	98	12.41%
	Never	448	56.71%

60. In the past twelve months I have drunk alcohol by myself

1-2 Times	63	7.97%
2-6 Times	43	5.44%
more than 6 times	23	2.91%
Never	654	82.78%

61. How much do … Books … influence how you think and act?

Not at all or Very Little	344	43.54%
Somewhat	341	43.16%
Very Much	96	12.15%

62. How much do … Friends … influence how you think and act?

Not at all or Very Little	38	4.81%
Somewhat	278	35.19%
Very Much	467	59.11%

63. How much does … Church Youth Group … influence how you think and act?

Not at all or Very Little	93	11.77%
Somewhat	321	40.63%
Very Much	365	46.20%

64. How much do … Parents … influence how you think and act?

Not at all or Very Little	34	4.30%
Somewhat	219	27.72%
Very Much	530	67.09%

65. How much do … Magazines … influence how you think and act?

Not at all or Very Little	439	55.57%
Somewhat	281	35.57%
Very Much	63	7.97%

66. How much do … Movies … influence how you think and act?

Not at all or Very Little	369	46.71%
Somewhat	316	40.00%
Very Much	98	12.41%

67. How much does … Music … influence how you think and act?

Not at all or Very Little	296	37.47%
Somewhat	312	39.49%
Very Much	175	22.15%

68. How much does … Religion … influence how you think and act?

Not at all or Very Little	36	4.56%
Somewhat	181	22.91%
Very Much	566	71.65%

69. How much does … School … influence how you think and act?

Not at all or Very Little	75	9.49%
Somewhat	328	41.52%
Very Much	380	48.10%

70. How much does … Television … influence how you think and act?

Not at all or Very Little	307	38.86%
Somewhat	369	46.71%
Very Much	106	13.42%

71. How much does … The Internet … influence how think and act?

Not at all or Very Little	534	67.59%
Somewhat	191	24.18%
Very Much	56	7.09%

72. How much do … Computers … influence how you think and act?

Not at all or Very Little	460	58.23%
Somewhat	229	28.99%
Very Much	94	11.90%

73. How much do … Church School Teachers … influence how you think and act?

Not at all or Very Little	246	31.14%
Somewhat	365	46.20%
Very Much	170	21.52%

74. How much does … Pastor … influence how you and act?

Not at all or Very Little	94	11.90%
Somewhat	341	43.16%
Very Much	347	43.92%

75. How much do … Church Youth Workers (Teen Advisors) … influence how you think and act?

Not at all or Very Little	201	25.44%
Somewhat	340	43.04%
Very Much	236	29.87%

76. How much do … School Teachers … influence how you think and act?

Not at all or Very Little	173	21.90%
Somewhat	404	51.14%
Very Much	205	25.95%

77. How much does … Guidance Counselor … influence how you think and act?

Not at all or Very Little	377	47.72%
Somewhat	275	34.81%
Very Much	129	16.33%

78. Greatest problems you face:

	First	Second	Third	Weighting
Drug Abuse	7	5	5	36
Fear of War	6	13	10	54

	First	Second	Third	Weighting
Fears	59	59	55	350
Getting along with Parents	58	70	36	350
Peer Pressures	53	46	52	303
Career uncertainties	52	60	63	339
Concern About AIDS	5	9	5	38
Alcohol Abuse	5	6	15	42
Weight Problems	48	44	66	298
Teen Pregnancy	4	8	4	32
Economic Problems	4	7	18	44
Concern about STDs other than Aids	4	10	4	36
	27	41	24	187
Financing College	23	32	29	162
Depression	23	23	16	131
Growing Pains	20	20	40	140
Pressure to have sex	2	1	2	10
Homosexuality	151	112	54	731
School Grades	15	56	48	205
School Problems	11	17	43	110
Violence	107	46	62	475
Being Liked	0	3	0	6
Birth Control	0	1	3	5
Other	0	1	2	4
Abortion				

79. Greatest problems your best friend faces:

	First	Second	Third	Weighting
Getting along with Parents	82	73	59	451
Alcohol Abuse	7	21	24	87
Peer Pressures	63	58	79	384
Fear of War	6	2	7	29
Birth Control	5	5	8	33
Fears	32	52	37	237
Career uncertainties	31	39	33	204
Concern about STDs other than Aids	3	7	1	24
	3	3	11	26
Concern about AIDS	29	64	48	263
School Problems	21	22	26	133
Financing College	20	29	41	159
Pressure to have sex	20	29	28	146
Weight Problems	2	1	2	10
Abortion	19	28	26	139
Growing Pains	19	23	33	136
Depression	17	23	17	114
Drug Abuse	141	41	53	558
Being Liked	14	19	11	91
Teen Pregnancy	126	118	70	684
School Grades	11	14	32	93
Violence	10	9	17	65
Economic Problems	1	1	5	10
Homosexuality	1	1	4	9
Other				

80. Greatest problems facing people your age:

	First	Second	Third	Weighting
Fears	9	24	20	95
Drug Abuse	81	104	65	516
Peer Pressures	80	103	89	535
Violence	8	13	38	88
Concern About AIDS	7	10	7	48
Pressure to have sex	62	74	113	447
Concern about STDs other than Aids	6	7	26	58
	50	85	23	343
School Grades	47	55	48	299
Getting along with Parents	4	12	9	45
Financing College	36	58	51	275
Alcohol Abuse	3	4	2	19
Homosexuality	28	29	47	189
Teen Pregnancy	22	11	14	102
Career uncertainties	209	43	39	752
Being Liked	20	19	39	137

Depression	2	5	6	22
Economic Problems	2	5	2	18
Birth Control	2	1	1	9
Fear of War	2	0	5	11
Abortion	17	29	37	146
School Problems	14	25	33	125
Weight Problems	13	14	5	72
Growing Pains	1	0	0	3
Other				

81. Is it right/wrong to have an abortion for reasons other than saving the physical life of the mother

Not Sure	215	215
Right	36	36
Wrong	529	529

82. Is it right/wrong to have an abortion to save the physical life of the mother

Not Sure	325	41.14%
Right	298	37.72%
Wrong	157	19.87%

83. Is it right/wrong to have an abortion for any reason

Not Sure	257	32.53%
Right	21	2.66%
Wrong	500	63.29%

84. Is it right/wrong to have homosexual relationships

Not Sure	185	23.42%
Right	51	6.46%
Wrong	544	68.86%

85. Moral for two unmarried 16 year-olds who love each other to have sexual Intercourse

Not Sure	180	22.78%
Right	60	7.59%
Wrong	540	68.35%

86. Is it right/wrong to cheat on a test at school

Not Sure	147	18.61%
Right	20	2.53%
Wrong	614	77.72%

87. Is it right/wrong to lie to one's parent

Not Sure	127	16.08%
Right	15	1.90%
Wrong	638	80.76%

88. Is it right/wrong for sixteen-year-olds to drink a couple of beers at a party

Not Sure	249	31.52%
Right	52	6.58%
Wrong	480	60.76%

89. Is it right/wrong to steal clothes from a store that I know makes a lot of money

Not Sure	40	5.06%
Right	5	0.63%
Wrong	734	92.91%

90. Is it right/wrong for you to have sex with someone of the same sex as you

Not Sure	86	10.89%
Right	8	1.01%
Wrong	687	86.96%

91. Is it right/wrong for someone else to have sex with a person of the same sex as them

Not Sure	135	17.09%
Right	27	3.42%
Wrong	618	78.23%

92. Is Capital Punishment (Putting someone to for a crime they have committed)

Not Sure	322	40.76%
Right	164	20.76%
Wrong	296	37.47%

93. Is Euthanasia (Helping someone who is ill end their life to free them from suffering or because they are elderly and feel they have no more to offer) right/wrong

Not Sure	273	34.56%
Right	145	18.35%
Wrong	362	45.82%

94. Is it right/wrong to have sexual intercourse before you are married

Not Sure	204	25.82%
Right	44	5.57%
Wrong	534	67.59%

94. Is it right/wrong to have sexual intercourse before you are married

Not Sure	204	25.82%
Right	44	5.57%
Wrong	534	67.59%

95. Is it right/wrong when you are married to have a sexual relationship with someone other than the person you are married to

Not Sure	36	4.56%
Right	19	2.41%
Wrong	724	91.65%

96. Is it right/wrong to use birth control before you are

Not Sure	320	40.51%

married	Right	146	18.48%
	Wrong	313	39.62%
97. Is it right/wrong to look at pornographic material	Not Sure	230	29.11%
	Right	41	5.19%
	Wrong	502	63.54%
98. Is it right/wrong to have "cyber sex" with someone in a computer chat room on the Internet	Not Sure	178	22.53%
	Right	30	3.80%
	Wrong	570	72.15%
99. Is it right/wrong to help those who are less fortunate than you	Not Sure	25	3.16%
	Right	735	93.04%
	Wrong	19	2.41%
100. Is it right/wrong to help someone stand up against injustice, when you will not gain anything from doing so	Not Sure	117	14.81%
	Right	624	78.99%
	Wrong	37	4.68%
101. How many times in the past twelve months have you been out on a date (such as going to a party or movie with one person of the opposite sex)?	1-2 times	158	18.73%
	3-5 times	119	15.06%
	6-9 times	72	9.11%
	10-19 times	78	9.87%
	20 times or more	104	13.16%
	None	261	33.04%
102. Is it difficult for you to talk to other teens of the opposite sex?	No	672	85.06%
	Sometimes	12	1.52%
	Yes	103	13.04%
103. How often do you think about sex?	Never	135	17.09%
	Sometimes	490	62.03%
	Very Often	163	20.63%
104. Have you ever had sexual intercourse ("gone all the way" or "made love")?	I don't know what sexual intercourse is.	4	0.51%
	Never	705	89.24%
	Yes, 1 time	28	3.54%
	Yes, 2-5 times	18	2.28%
	Yes, 6 times or more	27	3.42%
105. Have you ever had sexual relations with someone of the same sex as you?	I don't know what sexual intercourse is.	6	0.76%
	Never	754	95.44%
	Yes, 1 time	6	0.76%
	Yes, 2-5 times	12	1.52%
	Yes, 6 times or more	8	1.01%
106. Have you ever been forced to have a sexual relation you did not want?	No	740	93.67%
	Yes	48	6.08%
107. Have you ever been sexually harassed?	No	615	77.85%
	Yes	173	21.90%
108. Teen Pregnancy - If you are a female, have you ever been pregnant, or if you are a male have you ever gotten someone pregnant?	No	716	90.63%
	Yes	9	1.14%
109. Do you have a teenage friend who has ever been pregnant and was not married at the time?	No	440	55.70%
	Yes	347	43.92%
110. Have you ever-considered committing suicide been pregnant and was not married at the time?	No	599	75.82%
	Yes	190	24.05%
111. Have you ever had an eating disorder?	No	667	84.43%
	Sometimes	4	0.51%
	Yes	117	14.81%
112. How much do you worry about …The violence around me?	Not at all or Very Little	173	21.90%
	Somewhat	432	54.68%
	Very Much	183	23.16%
113. How much do you worry about …Being discriminated against?	Not at all or Very Little	323	40.89%
	Somewhat	315	39.87%
	Very Much	148	18.73%
114. How much do you worry about …That I may take my	Not at all or Very Little	520	65.82%

own life?

	Somewhat	166	21.01%
	Very Much	100	12.66%
115. How much do you worry about …That I will be pressured into having sex before I am ready or against my will?	Not at all or Very Little	421	53.29%
	Somewhat	225	28.48%
	Very Much	139	17.59%
116. How much do you worry about …That I may have an eating disorder?	Not at all or Very Little	579	73.29%
	Somewhat	141	17.85%
	Very Much	67	8.48%
117. How much do you worry about …That I might commit suicide (kill myself).	Not at all or Very Little	629	79.62%
	Somewhat	107	13.54%
	Very Much	51	6.46%
118. How much do you worry about …That my parents will physically hurt me?	Not at all or Very Little	691	87.47%
	Somewhat	69	8.73%
	Very Much	27	3.42%
119. How much do you worry about …That I might die soon?	Not at all or Very Little	423	53.54%
	Somewhat	257	32.53%
	Very Much	108	13.67%
120. How much do you worry about …That I might not get into a good college?	Not at all or Very Little	246	31.14%
	Somewhat	310	39.24%
	Very Much	227	28.73%
121. How much do you worry about …That my parents will get divorced.	Not at all or Very Little	601	76.08%
	Somewhat	116	14.68%
	Very Much	65	8.23%
122. Are you an Orthodox Christian?	Yes	790	100%
123. How would you rate your Church Attendance:	a few times a month	93	11.77%
	I do not go tot Church	1	0.13%
	less than once a month	23	2.91%
	monthly	9	1.14%
	more than once a week	167	21.14%
	six times or less a year	6	0.76%
	weekly	484	61.27%
	yearly	4	0.51%
124. Do you feel close to your Church Community?	No	80	10.13%
	Sometimes	5	0.63%
	Yes	701	88.73%
125. What is your view of God?	Don't think there is a God	1	0.13%
	I know for sure that exists	621	78.61%
	Mostly sure that God exists	134	16.96%
	Not sure if God exists	29	3.67%
	I am sure there is no such thing as God	1	0.13%
126. Your view of Jesus?	A great man who lived long ago, but I do not think he was God	4	0.51%
	Great prophet, but not really the Son of God	1	0.13%
	Jesus was the Son of God but I doubt he rose from dead	11	1.39%
	Not sure that Jesus existed	4	0.51%
	The Son of God who became a man to save us. He died and rose from the dead	749	94.81%
	Was a man anointed by God at Baptism to be God's Son	12	1.52%
127. Do you believe there is a heaven where people who love God and have died are with God?	I am not sure Heaven exists	50	6.33%
	No	6	0.76%
	Yes	729	92.28%
128. Do you believe there is a hell where those who hate God and have died are in eternal	I am not sure Hell exists	149	18.86%
	No	38	4.81%
	Yes	601	76.08%
129. My religious beliefs greatly influence how I act at school and with my friends.	Most of the time	289	36.58%
	Rarely or never	108	13.67%
	Some of the time	388	49.11%
130. Church responds in a meaningful way to … Problems about drugs and alcohol?	No	337	42.66%
	Sometimes	4	0.51%
	Yes	442	55.95%

131. Church responds in a meaningful way to … Sexual Issues such as abortion and AIDS?	No	294	37.22%
	Sometimes	2	0.25%
	Yes	487	61.65%
132. Church responds in a meaningful way to … Problems of marriage and divorce?	No	205	25.95%
	Sometimes		
	Yes	575	72.78%
133. Church responds in a meaningful way to … Morality in government?	No	484	61.27%
	Sometimes	3	0.38%
	Yes	293	37.09%
134. Church responds in a meaningful way to … World problems, war and poverty?	No	262	33.16%
	Sometimes	3	0.38%
	Yes	517	65.44%
135. If you had a serious moral matter to discuss would you discuss it with … Your Pastor?	No	369	46.71%
	Sometimes	7	0.89%
	Yes	410	51.90%
136. If you had a serious moral matter to discuss would you discuss it with … Another Priest besides your pastor?	No	464	58.73%
	Sometimes	6	0.76%
	Yes	313	39.62%
137. If you had a serious moral matter to discuss would you discuss it with … Another adult in your parish	No	531	67.22%
	Sometimes	5	0.63%
	Yes	249	31.52%
138. If you had a serious moral matter to discuss would you discuss it with … A Church School Teacher	No	598	75.70%
	Sometimes	6	0.76%
	Yes	179	22.66%
139. If you had a serious moral matter to discuss would you discuss it with … Your Youth Group Advisor or Director?	No	488	61.77%
	Sometimes	9	1.14%
	Yes	283	35.82%
140. If you had a serious moral matter to discuss would you discuss it with … A teacher at school?	No	588	74.43%
	Sometimes	7	0.89%
	Yes	188	23.80%
141. If you had a serious moral matter to discuss would you discuss it with … A Friend?	No	99	12.53%
	Sometimes	7	0.89%
	Yes	680	86.08%
142. If you had a serious moral matter to discuss would you discuss it with … Your friend's parent?	No	609	77.09%
	Sometime	7	0.89%
	Yes	140	21.52%
143. If you had a serious moral matter to discuss would you discuss it with … An aunt or uncle?	No	448	56.71%
	Sometime	4	0.51%
	Yes	334	42.28%
144. If you had a serious moral matter to discuss would you discuss it with … No one?	No	680	86.08%
	Sometimes	6	0.76%
	Yes	91	11.52%
145. How important are your religious beliefs to you?	Fairly important	194	24.56%
	Not at all important	2	0.25%
	Not too important	14	1.77%
	Very important	572	72.41%
146. Clergyman has discussed: Capital Punishment	No	563	71.27%
	Sometimes	1	0.13%
	Yes	221	27.97%
147. Clergyman has discussed: Cloning	No	592	74.94%
	Yes	193	24.43%
148. Clergyman has discussed: Abortion	No	317	40.13%
	Sometimes	1	0.13%
	Yes	467	59.11%
149. Clergyman has discussed: Pre-marital sexual relations	No	282	35.70%
	Yes	503	63.67%
150. Clergyman has discussed: Birth control	No	554	70.13%
	Sometimes	1	0.13%

	Yes	231	29.24%
151. Clergyman has discussed: Adultery	No	337	42.66%
	Yes	449	56.84%
152. Clergyman has discussed: Euthanasia	No	577	73.04%
	Sometimes	2	0.25%
	Yes	205	25.95%
153. Clergyman has discussed: Homosexuality	No	419	53.04%
	Sometimes	1	0.13%
	Yes	366	46.33%
154. Have you ever attended Antiochian Village Camp in Pennsylvania?	No	323	40.89%
	Yes	464	58.73%
155. Did you enjoy Camp?	No	24	3.04%
	Yes	422	53.42%
156. Did you learn more about your Orthodox Faith while at Antiochian Village Camp?	No	17	2.15%
	Yes	431	54.56%
157. Would you go back to Antiochian Village Camp, if you had the opportunity?	Do not know	2	0.25%
	No	35	4.43%
	Yes	409	51.77%
158. Have you ever attended Camp St. Nicholas in Frazier Park, California?	No	674	85.32%
	Yes	110	13.92%
159. Did you enjoy Camp?	No	1	0.13%
	Yes	107	13.54%
160. Did you learn more about your Orthodox Faith while at Camp St. Nicholas?	No	9	1.14%
	Yes	99	12.53%
161. Would you go back to Camp St. Nicholas, if you had the opportunity?	No	3	0.38%
	Yes	105	13.29%
162. Have you attended an Orthodox Camp, other than the ones mentioned above in questions 154 and 158?	No	707	89.49%
	Yes	76	9.62%
163. Did you enjoy Camp?	No	6	0.76%
	Yes	67	8.48%
164. Did you learn more about your Orthodox Faith while at this Camp?	No	11	1.39%
	Yes	62	7.85%
165. Would you go back to this camp, if you had the opportunity?	No	11	1.39%
	Yes	61	7.72%
166. Have you ever attended your Regional Parish Life Conference?	No	242	30.63%
	Yes	546	69.11%
167. Did you enjoy the Regional Parish Life	No	11	1.39%
	Yes	481	60.89%
168. Did you learn anything new about your Orthodox Faith at this conference?	No	109	13.04%
	Yes	390	49.37%
169. Did you meet new Friends at this conference?	No	39	4.94%
	Yes	456	57.72%
170. Did you feel welcomed?	No	29	3.67%
	Sometimes	5	0.63%
	Yes	461	58.35%
171. If you have the opportunity, will you attend another Regional Parish Life Conference?	Maybe	1	0.13%
	No	12	1.52%
	Yes	478	60.51%
172. Are you a member of Teen SOYO or another Youth Group in your parish other than Church	No	125	15.82%
	Yes	656	83.04%
173. How comfortable do you feel in sharing your Orthodox Faith with others?	I will not share it	4	0.51%
	Not comfortable	27	3.42%
	Somewhat	304	38.48%
	Very Comfortable	447	56.58%
174. Would you recommend your church to a friend who does not belong to another Church?	No	34	4.30%
	Not Sure	142	17.97%

	Yes	605	76.58%
175. Do you feel that you have a relationship with God?	No	39	4.94%
	Sometimes	12	1.52%
	Yes	729	92.28%
176. Are you a convert to the Orthodox Church?	No	609	77.09%
	Yes	163	20.63%
177. Do you feel comfortable in the Orthodox Church you now attend?	No	40	5.06%
	yes	743	94.05%
178. Do you feel comfortable attending Regional Conferences and Retreats?	Never attended one	139	17.59%
	No	56	7.09%
	Yes	588	74.43%
179. Do you feel that the Ten Commandments are relevant to your life?	No	86	10.89%
	Sometimes	13	1.65%
	Yes	681	86.20%
180. Have others asked you to join a Church or Religious group, other than the Orthodox Church?	No	534	67.59%
	Yes	250	31.65%

If asked, which Church/Religion

A Youth Group	3	1.49%
all	1	0.50%
Assemblies of God	1	0.50%
Atheist	1	0.50%
Aunts & Uncles'	1	0.50%
Baptist	40	19.90%
Bible Study	1	0.50%
Born Again	3	1.49%
Campus Group	1	0.50%
Catholic & Protestants	1	0.50%
Charismatic	1	0.50%
Church of God	1	0.50%
Community Church	2	1.00%
CYC	1	0.50%
Disciples of Christ	1	0.50%
Episcopal	1	0.50%
Episcopal	1	0.50%
Evangelical	1	0.50%
Four Square Gospel	1	0.50%
Friend's Church	1	0.50%
Full Gospel,	1	0.50%
Jehovah Witness	29	14.43%
Logos	1	0.50%
Lutheran	5	2.49%
Maronite	1	0.50%
Methodist	3	1.49%
Mormon	18	8.96%
Nazarene Church	2	1.00%
Non-denominational	3	1.49%
not sure of name	1	0.50%
Presbyterian	11	5.47%
Protestant	15	7.46%
Protestant Youth	1	0.50%
Roman Catholic	1	0.50%
Roman Catholic	35	17.41%
Seventh Day	1	0.50%
several	1	0.50%
The Rock Church	1	0.50%
Van Hallaaschls	1	0.50%
Ward	1	0.50%
Wicken	1	0.50%
Young Life	4	1.99%

181. Has anyone ever asked you to join a cult?	No	729	92.28%
	Yes	43	5.44%

If asked, which Cult?

A Coven	1	3.33%
A Friend's Group	1	3.33%
Alfa	1	3.33%

Boy Scouts	1	3.33%
D & D	1	3.33%
devil worshipers	1	3.33%
Figt all girls cult	1	3.33%
friend's	1	3.33%
Heaven's Gate	1	3.33%
Jehovah Witness	3	10.00%
KKK	4	13.33%
Mormon	2	6.67%
Mormons	2	6.67%
Online Group	1	3.33%
our church SP & P	1	3.33%
Satanic	1	3.33%
WICCA	1	3.33%
Wicken	3	10.00%
Witchcraft	2	6.67%
York University	1	3.33%

182. Do you ever discuss your religion with your friends?

No	135	17.09%
Sometimes	3	0.38%
Yes	642	81.27%

183. Do your friends ever seriously challenge what you believe in?

No	483	61.14%
Yes	297	37.59%

184. Do your friends ever challenge your belief in Jesus Christ?

No	581	73.54%
Sometimes	2	0.25%
Yes	192	24.30%

185. Do you feel prepared to discuss your Orthodox Faith with your friends?

No	175	22.15%
Yes	599	75.82%

186. Rate how well you feel your church: Helps you learn about the Bible

Excellent	308	38.99%
Fair	31	3.92%
Good	280	35.44%
Okay	137	17.34%
Poor	20	2.53%

187. Rate how well you feel your church: Helps you learn what it means to be an Orthodox

Excellent	431	54.56%
Fair	26	3.29%
Good	230	29.11%
Okay	83	10.51%
Poor	6	0.76%

188. Rate how well you feel your church: Helps in meeting your spiritual needs?

Excellent	276	34.94%
Fair	43	5.44%
Good	297	37.59%
Okay	149	18.86%
Poor	8	1.01%

189. Rate how well you feel your church: Helps you in understanding today's problems?

Excellent	183	23.16%
Fair	79	10.00%
Good	264	33.42%
Okay	213	26.96%
Poor	28	3.54%

190. Rate how well you feel your church: Helps you learn what is special about you?

Excellent	178	22.53%
Fair	112	14.18%
Good	206	26.08%
Okay	214	27.09%
Poor	56	7.09%

191. Rate how well you feel your church: Helps your religious faith grow?

Excellent	383	48.48%
Fair	35	4.43%
Good	253	32.03%
Okay	92	11.65%
Poor	11	1.39%

192. Rate how well you feel your church: Helps you make friends?

Excellent	290	36.71%
Fair	59	7.47%
Good	214	27.09%
Okay	157	19.87%
Poor	53	6.71%

193. Rate how well you feel your church: Helps you to get to know adults who care about you?

Excellent	273	34.56%
Fair	81	10.25%
Good	218	27.59%
Okay	155	19.62%
Poor	46	5.82%

194. Rate how well you feel your church: Helps you to help other people?

Excellent	339	42.91%
Fair	36	4.56%
Good	251	31.77%
Okay	128	16.20%
Poor	20	2.53%

195. Rate how well you feel your church: Helps you learn about what is right or wrong?

Excellent	394	49.87%
Fair	32	4.05%
Good	249	31.52%
Okay	95	12.03%
Poor	4	0.51%

196. Rate how well you feel your church: Helps you learn about sex and sexual values?

Excellent	215	27.22%
Fair	84	10.63%
Good	196	24.81%
Okay	188	23.80%
Poor	88	11.14%

197. Rate how well you feel your church: Helps you learn about alcohol and other drugs, and what your values about them should be?

Excellent	174	22.03%
Fair	107	13.54%
Good	196	24.81%
Okay	211	26.71%
Poor	80	10.13%

198. Rate how well you feel your church: Provides lots of fun and good times?

Excellent	366	46.33%
Fair	26	3.29%
Good	251	31.77%
Okay	108	13.67%
Poor	20	2.53%

199. Rate how well you feel your church: Helps you learn what a Christian should do about big issues such as poverty, war, and loneliness.

Excellent	240	30.38%
Fair	70	8.86%
Good	232	29.37%
Okay	171	21.65%
Poor	55	6.96%

200. Rate how well you feel your church: Shows compassion and love to you.

Excellent	425	53.80%
Fair	39	4.94%
Good	212	26.84%
Okay	84	10.63%
Poor	6	0.76%

201. Rate how well you feel your church: Allows you as a teen to have a role in the ministry of the

Excellent	366	46.33%
Fair	38	4.81%
Good	223	28.23%
Okay	116	14.68%
Poor	20	2.53%

202. How often do you pray alone:

Frequently	381	48.23%
Hardly ever	74	9.37%
Never	13	1.65%
Occasionally	310	39.24%

203. Describe how often you normally attend Church Services

a few times a month	86	10.89%
I do not go tot Church	9	1.14%
less than once a month	26	3.29%
more than once a week	189	23.92%
Once a month	5	0.63%
weekly	466	58.99%

204. How often do you read the Bible?

Daily	41	5.19%
Less than monthly	294	37.22%
Monthly	131	16.58%
Never	162	20.51%
Weekly	152	19.24%

205. In the past 30 days have you watched any religious programs on television?

No	649	82.15%
Yes	132	16.71%

206. In the past 30 days have you listened to any religious programs on radio?

No	704	89.11%
Yes	76	9.62%

207. If I were having trouble in school, I would turn to:

Adult	1	0.13%
Adult friend/relative	17	2.15%
Coach	1	0.13%
Friend my own age	152	19.24%
God	2	0.25%
Nobody	29	3.67%
Parent	475	60.13%
Priest	1	0.13%
School Counselor	95	12.03%
Siblings	2	0.25%
Teacher	3	0.38%
Youth worker or advisor	1	0.13%

208. If I were wondering how to handle my feelings, I would turn to:

Adult	5	0.63%
Adult friend/relative	35	4.43%
"e"	2	0.25%
family	1	0.13%
Friend my own age	363	45.95%
God	4	0.51%
Grandfather	1	0.13%
Nobody	74	9.37%
On-line computer chat room	2	0.25%
Parent	220	27.85%
Priest	49	6.20%
School Counselor	13	1.65%
sibling	4	0.51%
Youth worker or advisor	8	1.01%

209. If some of my friends started using alcohol or other drugs, I would turn to:

Adult	14	1.77%
Adult friend/relative	72	9.11%
Church Members	1	0.13%
family	1	0.13%
Friend my own age	186	23.54%
God	4	0.51%
Nobody	143	18.10%
On-line computer chat room	2	0.25%
Parent	234	29.62%
Priest	38	4.81%
School Counselor	54	6.84%
sibling	5	0.63%
the ones using drugs	1	0.13%
Youth worker or advisor	24	3.04%

210. If I had a question about sex, I would turn to:

Adult	12	1.52%
Adult friend/relative	53	6.71%
anyone	1	0.13%
Friend my own age	231	29.24%
God	1	0.13%
health teacher	1	0.13%
Nobody	84	10.63%
On-line computer chat room	9	1.14%
Parent	314	39.75%
Priest	37	4.68%
School Counselor	13	1.65%
sibling	5	0.63%
Youth worker or advisor	16	2.03%

211. If I were feeling guilty about something I had done, I would turn to:

Adult friend/relative	19	2.41%
Friend my own age	213	26.96%
God	5	0.63%
Nobody	44	5.57%
On-line computer chat room	2	0.25%
Parent	192	24.30%
Priest	283	35.82%
School Counselor	3	0.38%
sibling	3	0.38%
someone	1	0.13%

107

	Youth worker or advisor	10	1.27%
212. If I were deciding what to do with my life, I would turn to:	Adult	6	0.76%
	Adult friend/relative	42	5.32%
	all	1	0.13%
	family	1	0.13%
	Friend my own age	68	8.61%
	God	6	0.76%
	Nobody	32	4.05%
	On-line computer chat room	1	0.13%
	Parent	534	67.59%
	Priest	32	4.05%
	School Counselor	46	5.82%
	Teacher	1	0.13%
	Youth worker or advisor	8	1.01%
213. If I were deciding whether it was right or wrong to have an abortion I would turn to:	Adult	4	0.51%
	Adult friend/relative	29	3.67%
	Does Not Apply	1	0.13%
	Friend my own age	64	8.10%
	God	3	0.38%
	grandfather	1	0.13%
	I would not have an abortion	9	1.14%
	myself	1	0.13%
	Nobody	77	9.75%
	On-line computer chat room	4	0.51%
	Parent	321	40.63%
	Priest	227	28.73%
	School Counselor	9	1.14%
	sibling	2	0.25%
	Youth worker or advisor	19	2.41%
214. If I were struggling with a moral or ethical issue I would turn to:	Adult	4	0.51%
	Adult friend/relative	27	3.42%
	all	1	0.13%
	all, except online chat	1	0.13%
	Church	1	0.13%
	Friend my own age	99	12.53%
	God	5	0.63%
	grandfather	1	0.13%
	Nobody	36	4.56%
	Not Sure	1	0.13%
	On-line computer chat room	3	0.38%
	Parent	360	45.57%
	Priest	201	25.44%
	School Counselor	7	0.89%
	sibling	1	0.13%
	Youth worker or advisor	26	3.29%

ORTHODOX CHRISTIAN TEEN SURVEY
Copyright © 1998-2002 by Archpriest Joseph Purpura of the Antiochian Orthodox Christian Archdiocese Department of Youth
http://www.antiochian.org/youth

+ Metropolitan Theodosius
Primate of the Orthodox Church in America
Chancery of the Orthodox Church in America
P.O. Box 675, Syosset, NY 11791 / USA
Tel: 1-516-922-0550 / Fax: 1-516-922-0954
info@oca.org—http://www.oca.org/

Sanctity of Life Sunday[109]
January 21, 1996
To the Venerable Hierarchs, Reverend Clergy, Monastics, and Faithful of the Orthodox Church in America

Dearly beloved,

The issue of abortion continues to divide Americans. Not since the War Between the States has our country been so polarized regarding the value and dignity of human life.

For over two decades both sides of the abortion controversy have waged aggressive campaigns of words and ideologies. Both sides ironically claim to defend the inalienable right of human freedom. Safeguarding their respective positions, they have drawn attention to life as it exists in or outside of the womb. To defend the unborn or to defend the mother is one of the questions that has helped to polarize our country.

The Orthodox Church teaches that human life is called to be the image and likeness of God. Its value, and therefore its dignity, cannot be determined solely by a legal mandate. The honor and glory of the human person is derived from his or her relationship with the Living God and the desire to embrace and commune with other human beings.

History has taught us that laws change—sometimes for the better and sometimes for the worse. Thus, when human behavior is dependent on the law of the land we can expect that in a democratic context laws, and therefore behavior, inevitably change. This presents one of the great challenges for contemporary Orthodoxy in America. Personally and corporately the Orthodox have a divine mandate to defend all human life. This defense does not preclude the use of our courts and legislature. Yet, the Orthodox Christian cannot allow himself to imagine that legislating morality is as lasting and binding as the spirit of repentance. Laws assert themselves by imposing their authority upon a body of citizens. They affect behavior but they do not necessarily change the mind and the heart—especially of those who do not agree with the law or who overtly oppose the law. Repentance, on the other hand, is ultimately an act of love for the living and Triune God. It is an act of freedom that liberates one from sin and death. Therefore, the sin of aborting cannot be remedied solely by the law, particularly when the law is motivated by party politics. The law can be useful only in so far as it may lead to a change of the mind and the heart—a move towards true repentance.

If the Orthodox Church is to speak with a clear and convincing voice—if it is to proclaim the saving truth in love—then it must be free from the ongoing and changing dynamics of partisan objectives. For Orthodox Christians the care and veneration of human life cannot have as its foundation the popular vote. Our Church is to offer the way to

---

[109] Metropolitan Theodosius, "Sanctity of Life," 21 January 1996, available at http://www.oca.org/OCA/Pastoral-Letters/1996-Sanctity-of-Life.html: Internet; accessed 5 March 1999.

repentance. It is to offer the way by which an inner change and transformation can occur in the context of true and everlasting freedom. For only with "a broken and contrite heart" (Psalm 51:17) comes the discovery that human life, originating at conception, is a divine gift called to participate in divine life. Only "a broken and contrite heart" can recognize that jeopardizing and destroying human life—human life originating at conception, is an open rebellion against the living God.

With a firm hand and a gentle heart let us proclaim the holiness of life. Let us seek to heal the division in our land by pointing the way to the community of the saints where life reigns for all eternity.

With love in Christ,

\+ THEODOSIUS
Archbishop of Washington
Metropolitan of All America and Canada

+ Mctropolitan Theodosius
Primate of the Orthodox Church in America
Chancery of the Orthodox Church in America
P.O. Box 675, Syosset, NY 11791 / USA
Tel: 1-516-922-0550 / Fax: 1-516-922-0954
info@oca.org—http://www.oca.org

Sanctity of Life Sunday [110]
January 18, 1998
To the Venerable Hierarchs, Reverend Clergy, Monastics, and Faithful of the Orthodox Church in America

---

Dearly beloved,

Our American society stands polarized over the issue of abortion. It has become a moral issue used for political leverage in the public arena. The Orthodox Church, however, continues to speak out against terminating life in the mother's womb. Orthodox Christians have always viewed the willful abortion of unborn children as a heinous act of evil. Abortion is an act of murder for which those involved will answer to God.

Orthodox Christians must not turn a blind eye to this moral and political issue. Orthodox Christians are to contribute to legislative processes regarding this issue. But Orthodox Christians must not respond to this issue merely as a moral or political one. Simply pointing out the deficiencies of present legislation regarding abortion or bemoaning the moral decay of our times is not enough. It is not sufficient simply to legislate morality. The Church must strive in *"truth and love"* to appeal to the human conscience, the very core of human existence, which ultimately transcends all political and ideological platforms. We must seek not only to change human laws, but also to convert human hearts. Preaching the *"Good News"* of the Gospel of Christ, we must strive to heal a divided community.

By appealing to the human conscience, to the very core of human existence, the Church, through her pastors and faithful, is called to bring all to the understanding that life is a gift from God which is to be nurtured and revered. Care for life in the womb must extend to all aspects of human existence and development. This compels the Church, and therefore all of our parishes, to be centers of prayer and learning—to be centers where the human conscience is in harmony with the Divine Will. This compels us to offer the compassion and forgiveness of Christ to all who repent for the neglect and abuse of human life.

With a prophetic voice the Church is to continue proclaiming to Her faithful and to all the world that human life, beginning at conception, is created by God to develop and participate in Divine Life. With a prophetic voice the Church must continue its mission to call a divided and scattered people into the unity of the Triune and Tripersonal God—the very source and goal of all life.

With love in Christ,

+ THEODOSIUS
Archbishop of Washington
Metropolitan of All America and Canada

---

[110] Metropolitan Theodosius, "Sanctity of Life," 18 January 1998, available at http://www.oca.org/OCA/Pastoral-Letters/1998-Sanctity-of-Life.html; Internet; accessed 5 March 1999.

+ Metropolitan Theodosius
Primate of the Orthodox Church in America
Chancery of the Orthodox Church in America
P.O. Box 675, Syosset, NY 11791 / USA
Tel: 1-516-922-0550 / Fax: 1-516-922-0954
info@oca.org—http://www.oca.org/

Sanctity of Life Sunday [111]
January 17, 1999
To the Venerable Hierarchs, Reverend Clergy, Monastics, and Faithful of the Orthodox Church in America

Dearly beloved,

On the verge of the new millennium, it is clear that our society is dreadfully confused regarding the matter of the sanctity of life. Truly, we must be grateful for the defense of human freedom in this society that allows us to freely exercise our Orthodox faith. Yet, we must also recognize that this defense of human freedom, when exercised outside of a proper understanding of the source and goal of human life, has led to certain unacceptable results and conclusions.

Our society—*in the name of a freedom, namely the freedom of choice*—has enshrined in law the premise that abortion is acceptable, and seems to be approaching the conclusion that suicide and even euthanasia may also be acceptable. Additionally, our society has mistakenly engaged in the self-indulgent glorification of human existence in this world, while at the same time cynically questioning whether human life has any ultimate value at all.

While our society may be confused about these issues, the Church is not. The source and goal of human life in this world has been revealed to us by God. We are blessed to know that life in this world is not an end in itself. We are also blessed to know that life in this world is only a beginning. The true value of life, the reason we call it holy, is that each and every person in his or her life is called to participate in the very existence of God. We strongly affirm that this participation begins from the very start of life in the mother's womb and continues through earthly life into eternal life. Human life is created by God, and has its beginning and end in God. The sanctity of life is discovered in that truth.

We must ceaselessly witness to the true value and place of human life. We must oppose the untimely termination of human life as being tragically contrary to our true calling. We must also oppose both the hedonistic glorification and the cynical reduction of life in this world. We must advocate and demonstrate the truly balanced approach to life that is witnessed to and manifested by the authentic Christian tradition in all its fullness.

As we strive to do this, we must be mindful of the reality of sin. Realizing our own sinfulness, we must, in Christ Jesus, offer the possibility of repentance and redemption to all: not only to those who have been wronged, but even more so to those who have acted

---

[111] Metropolitan Theodosius, "Sanctity of Life," 17 January 1999, available at http://www.oca.org/OCA/Pastoral-Letters/1999-Sanctity-of-Life.html; Internet; accessed 5 March 1999.

112

wrongly. This is especially true of those who have been involved, in any way, with the sinful act of the untimely termination of a human life.

Let us then, dearly beloved, *"exhort one another every day...[that none] may be hardened by the deceitfulness of sin. For we share in Christ, if only we hold our first confidence firm to the end"* (Heb. 3:13).

With love in Christ,

+ THEODOSIUS
Archbishop of Washington
Metropolitan of All America and Canada

Orthodox Church in America
Tenth All-American Council, July, 1992

Synodal Affirmations
On Marriage, Family, Sexuality,
and the Sanctity of Life[112]

Contents

- Introduction

- The Mystery of Marriage
  - Marriage and Sexuality
  - Divorce, Widowhood, and Remarriage
- The Procreation of Children
  - Abortion
- Celibacy and Virginity

- Parents and Children
  - Single Parent Families
  - Adoption
  - Abuse in Family and Society
- Homosexuality
- Sickness, Suffering, and Death

These affirmations on marriage, family, sexuality and the sanctity of life are issued by the Holy Synod of Bishops on the occasion of the Tenth All-American Council of the Orthodox Church in America.

Miami, Florida, July 1992

Introduction

The Orthodox Church in America, being, with all Orthodox Churches in the world, the one, holy, catholic and apostolic Church of Christ, acting upon her mandate to teach God's truth to all people, solemnly affirms that every human person is made in God's image and likeness for everlasting life in God's coming kingdom.

As the crown of God's good creation, redeemed by Christ and sanctified by the Holy Spirit, all men, women and children-young and old, sick and healthy, rich and poor, powerful and weak, educated and uneducated, born and unborn-are eternally precious in God's sight.

All human beings will be raised from the dead on the last day. Those who seek the truth, do good and follow

---

[112] "Orthodox Church in America: Synodal Affirmations on Marriage, Family, Sexuality, and the Sanctity of Life," July 1992. Reproduced with permission from http://www.oca.org/OCA/All-American-Council/10-Miami-1992/Synodal-Affirmations.html; Internet; accessed 5 March 1999.

God's law written on their hearts and fully revealed to the world in Jesus Christ, God's incarnate Word, will inherit everlasting life. Those who persist in their evil ways, following their own will, will be forever lost (cf. Romans 2:14-16; John 1:1-18, 5:25-30).

The Holy Synod of Bishops of the Orthodox Church in America, assembled in council with priests and elected parish lay delegates, is gravely concerned about the degradation of human life in our day. We are especially concerned about the desecration of marriage and family life, the vilification of celibacy and virginity, the perversion of human sexuality, the devaluation of human suffering, and the destruction of the natural environment. We therefore take this opportunity, being gathered at our Tenth All-American Church Council, to reaffirm the God-given vision of these elemental aspects of human being and life.

The Mystery of Marriage

God creates human beings in His own image and likeness, male and female. He declares human life, with all that He makes, to be "very good" (Genesis 1:27-31).

God wills that men and women marry, becoming husbands and wives. He commands them to increase and multiply in the procreation of children, being joined into "one flesh" by His divine grace and love. He wills that human beings live within families (Genesis 1:27; 2:21-24; Orthodox Marriage Service).

The Lord Jesus blessed marriage in which the "two become one flesh" when, by his presence with his mother Mary and his disciples at the marriage in Cana of Galilee, he revealed his messianic glory in his first public miracle, evoking for the first time the faith of his disciples (Genesis 2:24; John 2:1-11).

The Lord Jesus Christ abrogated the practice of divorce which was permitted in the old covenant due to the people's "hardness of heart," insisting that one unique marriage between man and woman was God's will from the beginning (Mark 10:2-9, Matthew 19:3-12). He stated clearly that "every one who divorces his wife, except on the ground of unchastity [porneia], i.e. sexual immorality], makes her an adulteress; and whoever marries a divorced woman commits adultery" (Matthew 5:32).

The Lord went even further to declare that people who look at others in order to lust after them in their hearts have "committed adultery" (cf. Matthew 5:27-30).

Christ's apostles repeat the teachings of their Master, likening the unique marriage between one man and one woman to the union between Christ and His Church which they experience as the Lord's very body and His bride (Ephesians 5:21-33; 2 Corinthians 11:2).

While condemning those who forbid marriage as an unholy institution, along with those who defile marriage through unchastity (1 Timothy 4:3, Hebrews 13:4), the apostles commend as "the will of God" that Christians, as examples for all human beings, "abstain from unchastity [porneia]" and know how to marry "in holiness and honor, not in the passion of lust like heathen who do not know God." They insist that "whoever disregards this [teaching] disregards not man but God, who gives His Holy Spirit" to those who believe (1 Thessalonians 4:3-8).

Husbands are commanded to be the heads of their wives as Christ is the head of the Church. They are called to love their wives as their very selves, as Christ loves the Church, giving themselves in sacrifice to their brides as to their own bodies. And wives are called to respect and reverence their husbands as the Church devotes itself to Christ with whom she too, like the wife with her husband, is "one flesh" (Ephesians 5:21-33; Orthodox Marriage Service).

The "great mystery" of marriage (Ephesians 5:32) is the most used image and symbol in the Bible for God's relationship with His People in the old and new testaments where the Lord is the husband and His people are His wife—so often unfaithful and adulterous (cf. Hosea, Jeremiah, Ezekiel, Song of Songs, Corinthians, Ephesians, et. al.). And the ultimate union between the Lord and those saved by Christ for eternal life in God's kingdom by the indwelling Holy Spirit is likened to the communion of marriage (Revelation 21-22).

Convinced of these God-revealed truths, we offer the following affirmations and admonitions for the guidance of the faithful:

Every human being of whatever religion, race, nationality or moral convictions is to be respected and valued as a creature of God with the potential for everlasting life in God's coming kingdom.

No human being, whatever his or her religion, race, nationality or moral convictions, is to be treated in a wicked, evil or unjust manner.

Orthodox Christians are to make supplications, prayers, intercessions and thanksgivings (lit. Eucharist) for all people. This, according to Christ and the saints, includes one's enemies, cursers and abusers, as well as persecutors of the Church, heathens and heretics (Luke 6:27-49; 1 Timothy 2:1-4; St John Chrysostom, On First Timothy, Homilies 6 and 7; St. John of Kronstadt, My Life in Christ).

Marriage and Sexuality

Marriage and family life are to be defended and protected against every open and subtle attack and ridicule.

Sexual intercourse is to be protected as a sacred expression of love within the community of heterosexual monogamous marriage in which alone it can be that for which God has given it to human beings for their sanctification.

Sexual love in marriage is to be chaste and pure, devoid of lewdness, lechery, violence and self-gratification.

Couples planning to marry are to be properly counseled and prepared to confront the challenges of the married life, being guided in the ways to find within family life the way to spiritual fulfillment and sanctity.

Divorce, Widowhood, and Remarriage

Victims of broken marriages are to be counseled to repent of the evils, which caused the failure their original marriages, and to seek God's mercy and guidance in transforming the defeat into spiritual victory.

Widows and widowers are to be counseled whenever possible, particularly in the absence of small children in need of care, to remain faithful to their departed spouses who are alive in the Lord, maintaining the nuptial unity of love to be fulfilled in the kingdom of God for which they were crowned as husband and wife.

Widowed and divorced persons who remarry do so not as their right but as recipients of a special gift of God's mercy to be accepted with repentance, gratitude and the firm intention faithfully to fulfill all that belongs to married life.

The Procreation of Children

The procreation of children in marriage is the "heritage" and "reward" of the Lord; a blessing of God (cf. Psalm 127:3). It is the natural result of the act of sexual intercourse in marriage, which is a sacred union through which God Himself joins the two together into "one flesh" (Genesis 1-2, Matthew 19, Mark 10, Ephesians 5, et. al.).

The procreation of children is not in itself the sole purpose of marriage, but a marriage without the desire for children, and the prayer to God to bear and nurture them, is contrary to the "sacrament of love" (Orthodox Marriage Service; St. John Chrysostom, On Ephesians, Homily 20).

Married couples are encouraged to abstain from sexual union at times for the sake of devotion to prayer (as, for example, on the eves of the Eucharist, and during Lenten seasons). They are to do so, however, only "for a season by agreement" since their bodies are not their own but belong to each other; and they are to "come together again lest Satan tempt" them (cf. 1 Corinthians 7:2-7).

God himself "knits together" the child conceived in the mother's womb, beholding its "unformed substance" as it is being intricately wrought before his all-knowing eyes (Psalm 139:13-18). The Lord Jesus himself was first acknowledged on earth by John the Baptist when both the Lord and His Forerunner were still embryos within their mothers' wombs (Luke 1:39-45).

Orthodox Christians have always viewed the willful abortion of unborn children as a heinous act of evil. The Church's canonical tradition identifies any action intended to destroy a fetus as the crime of murder (Ancyra, Canon 21; Trullo, Canon 91; St. Basil, Canon 2).

Convinced of these God-revealed truths, we offer the following affirmations and admonitions for the guidance of the faithful:

The procreation of children is to take place in the context of marital union where the father and mother accept the care of the children whom they conceive.

Married couples may express their love in sexual union without always intending the conception of a child, but only those means of controlling conception within marriage are acceptable which do not harm a fetus already conceived.

Married couples may use medical means to enhance conception of their common children, but the use of semen or ova other than that of the married couple who both take responsibility for their offspring is forbidden.

Abortion

Abortion is an act of murder for which those involved, voluntarily and involuntarily, will answer to God.

Those finding themselves confronted with tragic circumstances where the lives of mothers and their unborn children are threatened, and where painful decisions of life and death have to be made—such as those involving rape, incest, and sickness—are to be counseled to take responsible action before God, who is both merciful and just, to whom they will give account for their actions.

Women and men, including family members and friends of pregnant women considering abortions, are to be encouraged to resist this evil act, and be assisted in bearing and raising their children in healthy physical and spiritual conditions.

Women who have had recourse to abortion, men who have fathered aborted children, and others involved in cases of abortion, are to be provided with pastoral care, which includes recognition of the gravity of the act and assurance of the mercy of God upon those who repent of their sins.

Orthodox Christians are to contribute to legislative processes according to their knowledge, competence, ability and influence so that laws may be enacted and enforced which protect and defend the lives of unborn children while being sensitive to the complexities and tragedies of life in contemporary society.

Celibacy and Virginity

Together with the most positive affirmation of marriage and family life, the Orthodox Church also affirms that the Lord calls some men and women to a life of celibacy and virginity. The "angelic way" of monastic life is especially blessed for men and women "able to receive this" as those so "assigned" and "called" (cf. Matthew 19:10-12; 1 Corinthians 7).

The monastic vocation is identified in Orthodox tradition with the "good portion" of Mary who sat at Jesus' feet, listening to his teaching and contemplating his truth in purity of heart. It is the calling to men and women to live in singleness, solitude, stillness and spiritual struggle in service to God; the way, which the apostle Paul practically recommends as the "better" way, if God so wills, in this fallen world filled with temptations and trials.

Beginning with Mary the Virgin Mother of God and St. John the Forerunner and Baptist of the Lord- not to speak

119

of the Lord Jesus Christ himself- the Orthodox Church's liturgical calendar of saints is filled with righteous celibates, virgin martyrs, and men and women who followed the monastic way in purity and holiness of life.

Convinced of these God-revealed truths, we offer the following affirmations and admonitions for the guidance of the faithful:

Celibacy and virginity are also to be defended and protected from vilification and ridicule.

Monastic life is to be defended, protected and promoted in witness to life in God's coming kingdom where all holy men and women will be "like angels in heaven" (Matthew 22:30).

Parents and Children

Human beings are created and saved to be the children of God, sons of the Father in Christ the only Son, by the indwelling Holy Spirit (Luke 3:38, John 1:12, Romans 8:14-17, Galatians 4:1-7).

With God as our Father in Christ and the Spirit, the heavenly Jerusalem, already here present with us in the Church of Christ, "is our mother" (Galatians 4:26, Revelation 21:2-10). As St. Cyprian of Carthage has said, "A person cannot have God for his Father, who has not the Church for his mother" (On the Unity of the Church, 5).

Since every fatherhood in heaven and on earth takes its name from the fatherhood of God (Ephesians 3:14), fathers in domestic, ecclesial and monastic families, together with holy mothers, are called to mediate God's presence and action to their children. The sacraments of marriage and ordination as well as the rites of monastic tonsure and the installation of abbots and abbesses testify to this spiritual calling.

Fathers are commanded not to provoke their children to anger, but to love them and "to bring them up in the discipline and instruction of the Lord" (Ephesians 6:4). And children are commanded to honor their father and mother, and to obey their parents in all things which are godly, realizing as they mature spiritually that they belong ultimately to God's household, receiving their identity not from their flesh and blood parents, but from God (Ephesians 6:1-4. Colossians 18-21, Matthew 10:34-39; 12:46-50; 23:9; Luke 15:26, John 1:12-13; et. al.).

Convinced of these God-revealed truths, we offer the

following affirmations and admonitions for the guidance of the faithful:

The family of father, mother and children, with the extended family of grandparents, aunts, uncles and cousins, is to be supported and protected as the basic condition of life for human beings in the this world.

Children are to be provided with the fullest and deepest possible experience of secure family life and activity.

The family is not to be idolized as an end in itself, thereby becoming an obstacle rather than a means to healthy and holy spiritual life in communion with God in the Church.

Single Parent Families

Although normal family life consists of a father and a mother together with their children, the growing number of single parent families which exist due to death, divorce and desertion are to be supported and honored.

Attention is to be given to the special spiritual, social and economic needs of single parent families.

Provision is especially necessary for the presence of loving adults of the gender of the missing parent in the family's life and activities.

And special care and support is needed for the single parent to persevere in a life of sexual chastity and holiness.

Adoption

The adoption of children without families to care for them by married couples and single people capable of providing them with spiritual and material care is to be supported and honored.

The blessed action of providing foster care to needy children is also to be supported and praised.

Adoption, not abortion, is the answer to unwilled pregnancy. Unmarried mothers are to be encouraged and supported in bringing their conceived babies to term and offering them for adoption.

Not for any reason, however, and certainly not for making money, are children to be conceived in order to be given up for adoption.

Adoption procedures involving large sums of money, profit motivation and coercion of families and mothers to give up their children is to be soundly rejected and condemned.

Abuse in Family and Society

All forms of physical, spiritual, psychological and emotional abuse of men, women and children are to be condemned.

Parents, and adults generally, are to be assisted in learning to treat children properly, avoiding abusive behavior because of the children's smallness, weakness and dependency.

Although women and children may be abusive in their own right, they are for many reasons more often the victims of abuse by men rather than men's abusers. Special attention is therefore to be given to the issue of "battered women and children" in our society.

The Christian teaching of the "headship" of the husband and father in the family is not to be interpreted as supportive in any way of abusive behavior; nor is the traditional teaching about the need to discipline children.

Positions of authority in family and society, as well as in churches, can be used in abusive ways. Some examples are the refusal of leaders to be available, to listen and to communicate respectfully and openly with subordinates, and even with peers in similar leadership positions; the use by those in authority of material and economic threats and punishments against those having legitimate disagreements and differences; the unsound and unwarranted appeals on the part of those in authority to the right for love, respect and obedience from their subordinates, and even peers, in order to shame or silence those who question their policies and actions. Every means is to be taken to be aware of the abuse of authority by those in leadership positions, and to expose and correct it.

Those in authority and positions of leadership may themselves be abused by peers and subordinates through unjust criticism, uninformed judgments, ungrounded accusations, careless talk, malicious gossip, disrespect, disdain and outright disobedience. These forms of abusive behavior must also be exposed and eliminated in human communities, including families and churches.

Efforts are also to be made to eliminate the sources of rage, discontent and depression, which lead to abuse in families and social and religious groups. Some of these are racial, religious and ethnic hatreds and injustices; sexual and carnal titillation; the cultivation of unrealistic expectations and desires; the acceptance of false promises about possible possessions and achievements; and the misuse of drugs and alcohol.

Many of the causes of human abuse are found in television programs, films, music, advertising, and social, political, ethnic and religious demagoguery which, primarily to make money, cater to the baser and weaker aspects of human life in the fallen world. These also are to be identified, exposed and eliminated.

Homosexuality

Created to know God's divinity and power through creation, human beings have refused to acknowledge God, to honor and thank Him, and to obey his divine teachings. Through their rebellion "they became futile in their thinking and their senseless hearts were darkened" (Romans 1:21). Therefore, as the apostle Paul continues to teach, "God gave them up in the lusts of their hearts to impurity, to the dishonoring of their bodies among themselves...their women exchanged natural relations for unnatural, and the men likewise gave up natural relations with women and were consumed with passion for one another, men committing shameless acts with men and receiving in their own persons the due penalty for their error" (Romans 1:26-27).

Homosexual acts, like adulterous and incestuous behavior, are condemned in the law of Moses. Those who do these things, both men and women, are, according to God's law of the old covenant, to be put to death (Leviticus 18:6-23; 20:10-21).

According to the apostle Paul, those engaging in homosexual acts, with fornicators, adulterers, idolaters, thieves, the greedy, drunkards, revilers and robbers, will not inherit the kingdom of heaven. Christians come from all these categories of evildoers who have, voluntarily and involuntarily, been caught up in the sin of the world. They are those who through their personal repentance and faith in Christ, their baptism and chrismation, and their participation in Holy Communion, have been "washed...sanctified...and made righteous in the name of the Lord Jesus and in the Spirit of our God" (1 Corinthians 6:9-11; Orthodox Baptism and Chrismation Service).

Jesus teaches mercy and forgiveness for all sinners, but the Lord does not justify sin. When the Son of God pronounces divine pardon to those caught in evil he always charges the forgiven sinner to "go and sin no more" (John

8:11).

Convinced of these God-revealed truths, we offer the following affirmations and admonitions for the guidance of the faithful:

Homosexuality is to be approached as the result of humanity's rebellion against God, and so against its own nature and well-being. It is not to be taken as a way of living and acting for men and women made in God's image and likeness.

Men and women with homosexual feelings and emotions are to be treated with the understanding, acceptance, love, justice and mercy due to all human beings.

People with homosexual tendencies are to be helped to admit these feelings to themselves and to others who will not reject or harm them. They are to seek assistance in discovering the specific causes of their homosexual orientation, and to work toward overcoming its harmful effects in their lives.

Persons struggling with homosexuality who accept the Orthodox faith and strive to fulfill the Orthodox way of life may be communicants of the Church with everyone else who believes and struggles. Those instructed and counseled in Orthodox Christian doctrine and ascetical life who still want to justify their behavior may not participate in the Church's sacramental mysteries, since to do so would not help, but harm them.

Assistance is to be given to those who deal with persons of homosexual orientation in order to help them with their thoughts, feelings and actions in regard to homosexuality. Such assistance is especially necessary for parents, relatives and friends of persons with homosexual tendencies and feelings. It is certainly necessary for pastors and church workers.

Sickness, Suffering, and Death

From the very beginning of human life on earth the rebellion of men and women against God has resulted in sickness, suffering and death. This is the meaning of the story of Adam and Eve, and their children and descendents, found in the first chapters of the Bible (Genesis 1-11).

Jesus Christ has come to save the world. He has come to free human beings from the tyranny of sickness, suffering and death through the forgiveness and expiation of their sins by his own sinless suffering and death.

Jesus Christ is the Lamb of God who takes upon himself the sins of the world. He is the new and final Adam who comes from heaven to give human beings the opportunity to begin life over again by dying and rising in him, and being sanctified and sealed by his life-creating Spirit (John 1:29; 1 Corinthians 15).

Jesus Christ shows us that human suffering has redeeming and sanctifying significance. It can be the means of finding God in the fallen world, the means of purification from carnal passions, the means of enlightenment and communion with God for everlasting life.

Through Christ's death, death itself is destroyed and transformed. Man's "final enemy," the "wages of sin," has become through Christ's crucifixion the way into paradise for those who fight it to the end, who refuse to surrender to its power, who destroy its very foundations by faith in God and love for Him and His good creation which has been corrupted and polluted by the evils of men (1 Corinthians 15, Romans 6).

The whole of creation- all the plants and animals, fish and birds, rocks and planets- is "groaning in travail" as it "waits with eager longing for the revealing of the sons of God;" for in the final coming of Christ all of creation "will be set free from the bondage to decay and obtain the glorious liberty of the children of God" (Romans 8:18-21).

The apostle Paul tells us that "the sufferings of the present time are not worth comparing with the glory that is to be revealed to us" (Romans 8:18). He says that our earthly sufferings are but the "slight momentary affliction" which "is preparing us for an eternal weight of glory beyond all comparison" (2 Corinthians 4:17).

Christians are waiting for the salvation of the world in God's coming kingdom where the Lord "will render to everyone according to his works" (Romans 2:6). The apostle continues, "to those who by patience in well-doing seek for glory and honor and immortality, he will give eternal life; but for those who are factious and do not obey the truth, but obey wickedness, there will be wrath and fury. There will be tribulation and distress for every human being who does evil...but glory and honor and peace for every one who does good...for God shows no partiality" (Romans 2:7-11).

Convinced of these God-revealed truths we offer the

following affirmations and admonitions for the guidance of the faithful:

All efforts to heal physical and spiritual sickness, to alleviate physical and spiritual suffering, and to prevent physical and spiritual death are to be supported and defended.

Those who suffer, and those related to the suffering, are to be helped to find God in their affliction, and so to acquire the divine grace and power to transform their pain into a means of purification from evil, illumination from darkness and eternal salvation in the age to come.

Adequate health care is to be made available for all men, women and children regardless of their, race, religion, social status, or financial condition. Great care must be taken so that healing services are not restricted to the affluent or the apparently "deserving."

Extreme caution is to be exercised in decisions involving medical treatment, especially in the face of death. Extreme care is always in order to find the "royal path" between providing all necessary healing measures and merely prolonging the biological functioning of organs when human life is no longer possible, or even present.

Scientific research and experimentation are to be undertaken with extreme caution in order not to bring greater evils and sufferings to humankind in place of intended blessings.

The natural world is to be treated as the friend and servant of humanity. It is not to be raped, corrupted and polluted for purposes of power, pleasure or profit. It resources are to be used with respect and gratitude for the well-being of all people on the planet (see Message of the Primates of the Most Holy Orthodox Churches, 6. Phanar, March 15, 1992).

Human beings are to be reminded by every means that they are not isolated individuals but are members one of another who will give account to God and to their fellow creatures for their every thought, word and deed; and that their eternal destiny depends on what they have done with their lives on earth.

Gay Gene

Copied on April 25, 1999 from http://www.msnbc.com/news/261874.asp

Study casts doubt on 'gay gene'

Canadian research fails to replicate earlier U.S. work

MSNBC NEWS SERVICES

April 22—Researchers in Canada cast doubt on the idea of a "gay gene" on Thursday, saying they had been unable to find any genetic link between brothers who are homosexual. In 1993, Dr. Dean Hamer and colleagues at the U.S. National Cancer Institute provoked a worldwide furor when they reported they had found evidence of a "gay gene" in men.

IN THE EARLIER report, researchers concluded that 33 of 40 pairs of gay brothers shared a set of genetic markers in an area of the X chromosome known as Xq28. Based on the discovery of these markers, called DNA sequences, the researchers postulated that a gene in this location could explain some instances of male homosexuality.

But in a study published in this week's Science, George Rice and colleagues at the University of Western Ontario in London, Canada, said they studied more pairs of gay brothers and found no evidence that they shared some sort of mutation in that area.

They examined blood samples taken from 52 pairs of gay brothers and found that the rate of shared genetic markers at Xq28 was no higher than would have been expected by chance.

RESEARCH CONTINUES

Even though the researchers were not able to confirm Hamer's findings, Rice and his colleagues did not rule out other genetic links to homosexuality. He said his team is still looking for such evidence in other locations.

The researchers said it was possible there was another "gay gene," as the team only looked at one gene for its study.

Men, in addition to their 22 pairs of matched chromosomes, have one X and one Y chromosome. Women have two Xs.

Men inherit their X chromosomes from their mothers, and because they have just one copy, are vulnerable to genetic defects carried on the X chromosome such as color blindness and Fragile X syndrome, which causes a form of mental retardation.

Hamer's team had noted a tendency for homosexuality to run in the female line—men whose mothers had gay brothers also tended to be homosexual, the team reported. So it looked for an area on the X chromosome that might be involved. The team homed in on an area known as Xq28.

Studies dating back to the 1980s show some evidence that homosexuality might run in families.

One study on identical twins, who share more of their genes than regular siblings, found one twin was more likely to be gay if his twin was, and another study found homosexual men were more likely to have homosexual brothers even if they were not twins.

TOO SOON FOR CONCLUSIONS

Another scientist who has conducted research on the subject said it is too early to make a final decision.

"I don't think that Rice's paper rules out that there could be an important gene in this area," said Dr. Alan Sanders, an assistant professor of psychiatry at the University of Chicago.

When scientists try to reproduce the findings of another research team, the results can be complicated, according to Sanders. Sometimes the second study arrives at the same conclusion, which bolsters the original idea. Other times the research contradicts the earlier work, Sanders said.

"We've got to wait and see," he said, adding that studies that involve larger numbers of participants should help to produce more definitive findings.

The Medical Tribune News Service and Reuters contributed to this report.

Hippocratic Oath

5th Century BC

I swear by Apollo the physician, AEsculapius, and Health, and All-heal, and all the gods and goddesses, that, according to my ability and judgment, I will keep this Oath and this stipulation—to reckon him who taught me this Art equally dear to me as my parents, to share my substance with him, and relieve his necessities if required; to look up his offspring in the same footing as my own brothers, and to teach them this art, if they shall wish to learn it, without fee or stipulation; and that by precept, lecture, and every other mode of instruction, I will impart a knowledge of the Art to my own sons, and those of my teachers, and to disciples bound by a stipulation and oath according the law of medicine, but to none others. I will follow that system of regimen which, according to my ability and judgment, I consider for the benefit of my patients, and abstain from whatever is deleterious and mischievous. I will give no deadly medicine to any one if asked, nor suggest any such counsel; and in like manner I will not give a woman a pessary to produce abortion. With purity and with holiness I will pass my life and practice my Art. I will not cut persons laboring under the stone, but will leave this to be done by men who are practitioners of this work. Into whatever houses I enter, I will go into them for the benefit of the sick, and will abstain from every voluntary act of mischief and corruption; and, further from the seduction of females or males, of freemen and slaves. Whatever, in connection with my professional practice or not, in connection with it, I see or hear, in the life of men, which ought not to be spoken of abroad, I will not divulge, as reckoning that all such should be kept secret. While I continue to keep this Oath unviolated, may it be granted to me to enjoy life and the practice of the art, respected by all men, in all times! But should I trespass and violate this Oath, may the reverse be my lot![113]

Note from Encarta Encyclopedia

Hippocratic Oath, oath of which varying versions have been taken for 2000 years by physicians entering the practice of medicine. At one time the oath was thought to come from ancient Greek physician <u>Hippocrates,</u> but modern research has shown that it most probably originated in a Pythagorean sect of the 300s BC. In its original form, the oath prohibited participation in surgery or abortions. At the height of Christianity, most European physicians accepted both of these prohibitions. Many contemporary medical schools impose a revised and modernized version of the oath as an admonition and an affirmation to which their graduating classes assent.[114]

Date unknown:

The Hippocratic Oath
Modern Version from Eastern Virginia Medical School

Upon this day of graduation from the Eastern Virginia Medical School, as I seek admission to the medical profession:

I do solemnly affirm, as did the ancient Greeks, by all that I hold most sacred that, according to my ability and judgment I will keep this oath and its stipulations.

I hold my teachers in this art are equal to my own parents and extend to them the respect and gratitude which is their due.

I will by precept, lecture, and every other mode of instruction impart a knowledge of the art to my progeny and those of my teachers, and to disciples bound by covenant and oath according to the law of medicine.

I will follow that system of treatment which according to my ability and judgment, I consider for the benefit of my patients and abstain from whatever is deleterious and mischievous.

I will exercise my art solely for cure of my patients and the prevention of disease and will give no drugs and perform no operations for a criminal purpose nor far less suggest such a thing.

With honor and dignity I will practice my profession not permitting consideration of religion, nationality, race or social standing to intervene between duty and my patient.

Into whatsoever houses I enter, I will go for the benefit of the sick and will hold myself aloof from every voluntary act of wrongdoing or corruption.

Whatever I may see or hear in the lives of others which ought not be spoken abroad, I will not divulge, reckoning that such should be kept secret.

---

[113] http://weber.u.washington.edu/~aed/oath.html
[114] http://encarta.msn.com/index/conciseindex/15/015b2000.htm

While I continue to keep this oath unviolated, may it be granted to me to enjoy life and the practice of the art, respected by all people in all times. But should I trespass and violate this oath, may the reverse be my lot.[115]

The following information was gathered concerning the British Medical Association proposed changes to the Hippocratic oath:

While it is common knowledge among both doctors and the lay public that doctors take an oath that says, "Never do harm," the fact is that not all medical schools require their graduating doctors take the Hippocratic Oath. In addition, Medicine's use of the Oath changes over time. Here are some items for your consideration, the results of a study by Robert Orr, M.D. and Norman Pang, M.D., in which 157 deans of allopathic and osteopathic schools of medicine in Canada and the United States were surveyed regarding the use of the Hippocratic Oath:

1. In 1993, 98 percent of schools administered some form of the Oath.
2. In 1928, only 26 percent of schools administered some form of the Oath.
3. Only 1 school used the original Hippocratic Oath.
4. 68 schools used versions of the original Hippocratic Oath.
5. 100% of current Oaths pledge a commitment to patients.
6. Only 43% vow to be accountable for their actions.
7. 14% include a prohibition against euthanasia.
8. Only 11% invoke a deity.
9. 8% prohibit abortion.
10. Only 3% prohibit sexual contact with patients.

From - "The Use of the Hippocratic Oath: A Review of 20th Century Practice and a Content Analysis of Oaths Administered in Medical Schools in the U.S. and Canada in 1993." by Robert D. Orr, M.D. and Norman Pang, M.D.
UPDATE
The British Medical Association, in March 1997, published their first draft of a revised Hippocratic Oath to be considered by the World Medical Association.
"The Oath, a set of ethical principles derived from the writings of the ancient Greek physician Hippocrates, has been updated to put patients first. It aims to be a unifying force, superseding national, ethnic, religious and cultural boundaries by focusing on widely shared values.
The new wording can be adapted by nurses, paramedics and other health professionals."
Commenting on the revised wording, Dr Sandy Macara, chairman of the BMA Council, said:

"It is as important now as ever it was for doctors to have an agreed statement of ethical principles. On qualifying, doctors need such a statement to make a public commitment to the professional responsibilities they are assuming. Thereafter these principles should provide

---

[115] http://users.exis.net/~finesre/2001/hippo1.htm

guidance in the increasingly difficult ethical decisions they will make throughout their professional lives.

"The value of this update will be all the greater if it comes into use by every doctor qualifying from every medical school in the world."

The BMA has been campaigning for the past five years for a revitalization of the Hippocratic values. It has gathered examples of ethical codes from all over the world and common points from these have been integrated into the new wording.

The BMA has undertaken this work on behalf of the World Medical Association as the first stage of a revision of the current international code of medical ethics, the Geneva Declaration, which celebrates its 50th anniversary next year.

Appendix I

DRAFT REVISION OF THE HIPPOCRATIC OATH
British Medical Association, March 1997

The practice of medicine is a privilege which carries important responsibilities. All doctors should observe the core values of the profession which centre on the duty to help sick people and to avoid harm. I promise that my medical knowledge will be used to benefit people's health. They are my first concern. I will listen to them and provide the best care I can. I will be honest, respectful and compassionate towards patients. In emergencies, I will do my best to help anyone in medical need.

I will make every effort to ensure that the rights of all patients are respected, including vulnerable groups who lack means of making their needs known, be it through immaturity, mental incapacity, imprisonment or detention or other circumstance.

My professional judgment will be exercised as independently as possible and not be influenced by political pressures nor by factors such as the social standing of the patient. I will not put personal profit or advancement above my duty to patients.

I recognize the special value of human life but I also know that the prolongation of human life is not the only aim of healthcare. Where abortion is permitted, I agree that it should take place only within an ethical and legal framework. I will not provide treatments which are pointless or harmful or which an informed and competent patient refuses.

I will ensure patients receive the information and support they want to make decisions about disease prevention and improvement of their health. I will answer as truthfully as I can and respect patients' decisions unless that puts others at risk of harm. If I cannot agree with their requests, I will explain why.

If my patients have limited mental awareness, I will still encourage them to participate in decisions as much as they feel able and willing to do so.

I will do my best to maintain confidentiality about all patients. If there are overriding reasons which prevent my keeping a patient's confidentiality I will explain them.

I will recognize the limits of my knowledge and seek advice from colleagues when necessary. I will acknowledge my mistakes. I will do my best to keep myself and colleagues informed of new developments and ensure that poor standards or bad practices are exposed to those who can improve them.

I will show respect for all those with whom I work and be ready to share my knowledge by teaching others what I know.

Joseph F. Purpura

I will use my training and professional standing to improve the community in which I work. I will treat patients equitably and support a fair and humane distribution of health resources. I will try to influence positively authorities whose polices harm public health. I will oppose polices which breach internationally accepted standards of human rights. I will strive to change laws which are contrary to patients interests or to my professional ethics. [116]

---

[116] http://www.imagerynet.com/hippo.ama.html

SELECTIVE BIBLIOGRAPHY

Antiochian Orthodox Christian Archdiocese of North America. *The Liturgikon: The Book of Divine Services.* New York: Athens Printing Company, 1989.

Barna Research Group. *Today's Teens: A generation in Transition.* Glendale, CA: The Barna Research Group, 1991.

Bartholomew I, Ecumenical Patriarch. "Stewards of Creation." *The Orthodox Church,* September/October 1997. Volume 33 - 9/10. 3.

Benson, Peter L. *The Troubled Journey: A Portrait of 6th-12th Grade Youth.* Minneapolis: Search Institute, 1993.

Berzonsky, Father Vladimir. *"Far away places." The Orthodox Church,* September/October 1997. Volume 33 - 9/10. 3.

Bezilla, Robert. Americas' Youth in the 1990s. Princeton, New Jersey: The George H. Gallup International Institute, December 1993.

Bromiley, Geoffrey W., Ed. *The International Standard Bible Encyclopedia Volume One - A-D.* Grand Rapids: William B. Eerdmans Publishing Company, 1979.

Chrysostom, St. John. *St. John Chrysostom on Marriage and Family Life.* Ed. Catherine P. Roth and David Anderson, trans. Crestwood, New York: St. Vladimir's Seminary Press, 1986.

Coalition for America's Children. "Kidscampaigns." 10-8-97. http://www.kidscampaigns.org/.

Englehardt Jr., H. Tristram. *Christian Bioethics: Non-Ecumenical Studies in Medical Morality.* Volume 4, Number 1 April 1998 Netherland: Swets & Zeitlinger, 1998.

_____. Christian Bioethics: Non-Ecumenical Studies in Medical Morality. Volume 4, Number 2, August 1998. Netherland: Swets & Zeitlinger, 1998.

Faith Worx Electronic Reference Library (CD), version 2.0. Theologic Systems. http://www.theologic.com, 1998.

Gallup, George H. Jr. *The Gallup Survey on Teenage Suicide.* Princeton, New Jersey: The George H. Gallup International Institute, December 1991.

_____. The Religious Life of Young Americans. Princeton, New Jersey: The George H. Gallup International Institute, December 1992.

Grassi, Joseph A. "Child, Children." *The Anchor Bible Dictionary Volume 1 A-C,* (New York, DoubleDay) 1992.

Kowalczyk, Rev. Fr. John. *An Orthodox View of Abortion.* Minneapolis, Minnesota: Gopher State Litho Co., 1977.

Leffert, Nancy, Ph.D., Rebecca N. Saito and Candyce H. Kroenke. *Making the Case: Measuring the Impact of Youth Development Programs.* Minneapolis: Search Institute, 1996.

Meyendorff, John. *Marriage: An Orthodox Perspective.* Crestwood, New York: St. Vladimir's Seminary Press, 1975.

Nassar, Reverend Seraphim. *Divine Prayers and Services of the Catholic Orthodox Church of Christ.* Englewood, NJ: Antiochian Orthodox Christian Archdiocese of North America, 1979.

St. Vladimir's Seminary Quarterly. Volume 25, Number 1, 1981. Crestwood, New York: St. Vladimir's Seminary Press, 1981.

Purpura, Joseph. *Teen Profile: Antiochian Orthodox Christian Archdiocese.* Westwood, MA: Department of Youth, 1992.

Roehlkepartain, Eugene C. *Building Assets in Congregations: A Practical Guide for Helping Youth Grow Up Healthy.* Minneapolis: Search Institute, 1998.

Roehlkepartain, Eugene C., and Margaret R. Hinchey. *Youth Ministry that Makes a Difference: 30 Keys to Strengthening Your Congregations Youth Ministry.* Minneapolis: Search Institute, 1997.

Roehlkepartain, Eugene C., and Dr. Peter C. Soales. *Youth Development: An Exploration of the Potential and Barriers In Congregations.* Minneapolis: Search Institute, 1995.

Roehlkepartain, Jolene L. Youth Ministry: Its impact in Church Growth. Loveland, Colorado: Group Publishing, 1990.

Stanley Samuel Harakas. *Contemporary Moral Issues: Facing the Orthodox Christian.* Minneapolis, Minnesota: Light and Life Publishing Company, 1982.

_____. *Living The Faith: The Praxis of Eastern Orthodox Ethics,* Minneapolis, Minnesota: Light and Life Publishing Company, 1992.

_____. *Toward Transfigured Life.* Minneapolis, Minnesota: Light and Life Publishing Company, 1983.

Rodger, Lynlea. "The Infancy Stories of Matthew and Luke." *Horizons in Biblical Theology* Volume 19 Number 1. June 1997. 58-62.

Shelley, John C. "Ethics in the New Testament." Mercer Dictionary of the Bible.

U.S. Government Census Bureau. "Web Site." 10-8-97. http://www.census.gov/.

Verhi, Allen D., article on Ethics. *The Oxford Companion to the Bible.* Ed. Bruce M. Metzger. New York: Oxford University Press, 1993.

ABOUT THE AUTHOR

The Very Rev Dr Joseph F Purpura is Chairman of the Department of Youth Ministry of the Antiochian Orthodox Christian Archdiocese of North America. He is a graduate of Iona College (B.A.), St Vladimir's Orthodox Theological Seminary (M.Div.), Yale Divinity School (S.T.M.) and Pittsburgh Theological School (D.Min.). Joseph Purpura has worked with Teens in the Church Setting since 1978. He is the father of four children, all of whom are in or have passed through the teen years, as of the writing of this book. This book reflects his insights and research spanning over the past twenty-four years of youth ministry experience.

Printed in the United States
by Baker & Taylor Publisher Services